C0-AOA-425

Seeing

❧

the

❧

Newspaper

❧

❧

❧

❧

Seeing the

NEWSPAPER

KEVIN G. BARNHURST

Syracuse University

ST. MARTIN'S PRESS
New York

EDITOR: Jane Lambert
MANAGING EDITOR: Patricia Mansfield-Phelan
PROJECT EDITOR: Talvi Laev
PRODUCTION SUPERVISOR: Patricia Ollague
ART DIRECTOR: Sheree Goodman
TEXT DESIGN: Patrice Fodero
COVER DESIGN: SG Design

Library of Congress Catalog Card Number 92-62727
Copyright © 1994 by St. Martin's Press, Inc.
All rights reserved. No part of this book may be reproduced, stored in a retrieval system, or transmitted by any form or by any means, electronic, mechanical, photocopying, recording, or otherwise, except as may be expressly permitted by the applicable copyright statutes or in writing by the Publisher.
Manufactured in the United States of America.

8 7 6 5 4
f e d c b a

For information, write:
St. Martin's Press, Inc.
175 Fifth Avenue
New York, NY 10010

ISBN: 0-312-06149-8 (paperback); 0-312-10800-1 (hardcover)

Library of Congress Cataloging-in-Publication Data applied for.

ACKNOWLEDGMENTS

Figure 1.1, reprinted by permission of the Andy Warhol Foundation for the Visual Arts.

Figure 1.2, from *The Newspaper Everything Book* by Vivienne Eisner and Adelle Weiss. Copyright © 1975 by Vivienne Eisner and Adelle Weiss. Used by permission of Viking Penguin, a division of Penguin Books USA Inc.

Figure 1.3, courtesy of Vis-Com Inc.

Figure 1.4, courtesy of *The Midland [Texas] Reporter-Telegram.*

Figure 2.1, from the author's collection.

Figure 2.2, copyright © 1993 C. Herscovici/ARS, New York.

Figure 2.3, courtesy of the Library of Congress.

Figure 2.4, reprinted by permission of The Peabody Museum of Archeology and Ethnology.

Figure 2.5, from *The New York Journal,* June 26, 1905, p. 1.

Figure 2.6, courtesy of Leica Camera, Inc.

Figure 2.7, installation view of the exhibition From the Picture Press, January 30–April 29, 1973. The Museum of Modern Art, New York. Photograph courtesy of The Museum of Modern Art, New York.

Figure 2.8, John Baldessari, *Wrong,* 1967. Courtesy of Los Angeles County Museum of Art.

Acknowledgments and copyrights are continued at the back of the book on page 215, which constitutes an extension of the copyright page.

PREFACE

Like many youngsters, I went on a tour of a newspaper's

premises with my class at school. My most vivid recollections

are of two places. One was the room with the gigantic presses,

hidden deep in the heart of the Tribune building, behind the

unpretentious façade on Main Street in Salt Lake City. The

noise was thunderous, and the speed, almost violent, was numbing,

as the paper flew through the pressuring rollers. The smell was one I will never forget—a smell of printer's ink, the heat of the room, and something else I later learned was molten lead. We trailed through the building until we came to another impressive place: the newsroom, a busy expanse of mostly men at desks with typewriters, stacks of yellowing paper, and wastebaskets. But we passed by the art department, with its oddly dressed artists tucked inconspicuously away.

Many years later, the columnist David Wilson took me through the premises of the *Boston Globe*, which had undergone two revealing changes. A new set of chemical fumes had replaced the acrid odor of lead in the pressroom, where the letterpress machines had been upgraded. The new offset equipment now outgrew the building. A glass enclosure made the machinery visible from Morrissey Boulevard, like the flap early medical researchers had opened to observe the stomach. The other change was in the newsroom, where the manual typewriters had been replaced. Although the standard key caps remained, the computer had absorbed, one by one, all of the older procedures and methods of producing news. The pencil of the copy editor, the hands of the typesetter, the droning voices of proofreaders, and, in some printing plants, the eyes of the camera operator, stripper, and platemaker have become one in the all-seeing eye of the video display terminal. If some predictions come true, even the presses, once the heart of newspapers, will also fall victim (Fidler). All of these processes, which were at one time muscular and mental, as well as mechanical, collapse into the whir and moan of the CPU in its air-conditioned cubicle.

It is customary to assign to the machinery the blame or applause for changing the newspaper from what it was to what it now is. But what occurred was technological only in its expression. The real impulse behind the changes was human and, specifically, artistic. At the *Globe*, the art department has moved to the new wing, on the other side of the building with the corporate offices. The artists—as many women as men, now—still wear unconventional clothes, but these are slick and trendy, worn with the patina of corporate efficiency, as if the wearers were leading the newspaper instead of hanging on at some extremity.

Not only did the artists move from the peripheral synapses to the nerve center of the *Globe*, the visual also colonized all the procedures and conceptions of news and the newspaper. In place of the relatively simple world where reporters hammered out real-life stories on machines, the newspaper has become a layered, multidimensional world in which journalists arbitrate among the many claims to represent the culture. Readers and journalists have come to think of news as consciously constructed rather than as a mechanical expression of truth. Political studies of the U.S. presidential elections have led to broad public debates that define journalism as image making (or image mongering). The change in the attitude toward news resulted less from a sudden technical advance than from the gradual infusion of art into journalism (or the venturing of journalism into the visual realm). The news arrayed on the front page is now like a painting, a version of events seen from the perspective of the journalist's art.

The Graphic Arts

Since journalism schools first appeared, a few typographers-turned-professors have introduced students and newspaper workers to the practical arts of making up and printing pages. Their lowly, applied field, which slowly grew to encompass other media such as magazines and advertising, shared a name with its more respected cousins, fine bookmaking and art printmaking. In the last decade, the graphic arts of mass communication have seen dozens of books and articles published, many of them cited in these pages: book-length histories and critical analyses, essays and scientific studies, collected visual works of contest winners and others, college textbooks and how-to manuals. The outpouring has changed a dime-store discipline into a strip mall of boutiques.

The changes in the graphic arts at newspapers and in the universities have made this book necessary. In these pages, I have tried to describe and map out what has been published, so that journalists and readers need not make or see the newspaper without some sense of its visual history and meaning. I have also attempted to introduce the ideas from philosophy, science, and art that contribute to a visual understanding of newspapers. This book supplements the many fine textbooks and illustrated manuals that provide encyclopedic technical information, myriad current and historical examples, and step-by-step instructions. It can also serve as a guide for those who wish to enter what has become a large and diverse literature outside the handbooks.

The field of graphic arts has traditionally maintained the boundaries between functions such as editorial and advertising and between forms such as magazines and newspapers. A shrewd writer might have cut a broader swath through the communications media, but I believe my reasons for not doing so are compelling. I have focused on newspaper journalism not only because it is what I know best. Television is arguably more important in mass culture, and advertising occupies more than half of newspaper pages and tends to dominate even when taking up less space. If anything, the role of the visual in these media is obvious. Newspaper design is another matter. In the past, news designs were stubbornly retrograde, and that makes their transformation all the more interesting. The ideas invading these least visual of forms take on even more significance in the context of advertising and help to explain the other visual media such as television. This book points out some implications while leaving a fuller discussion of advertising and television for a later work.

Even what is called the news and editorial side of the newspaper proved too large a topic for exhaustive treatment in a single volume. In fact, an entire book might be written on the subject of each chapter included here. These essays can only introduce the main arguments in the literature and point to ideas for further study. Space did not permit the inclusion of several important topics originally planned for the book. Newspaper illustration and editorial cartooning deserve attention and sustain an extensive field of research and writing. The study of color in newspapers is another essay that demands writing. An equally interesting chapter could cover logos, nameplates, and the other marks of identity that newspapers use. All of these visual means of understanding and enjoying the news had to be left for another study.

But limitations often turn out to impose a virtue. Channeling a wealth of ideas from many fields through the funnel of a few aspects of news-editorial design has been at once more rigorous and less confining because it opens the graphic arts—formerly the arcane interest of a few editors and publishers—to the whole audience of readers. Although not a universal public, newspaper readers are often passionately committed. Focusing on you, the reader, has forced my discussion to remain concrete, fervid, and close to home. In that spirit, several chapters ask that you take up a camera, your pencil, or the newspaper itself. Even if you will never help put out a newspaper, the experience of making pictures, counting up charts, identifying a typographic style, and so forth will let you test ideas against experience.

The practical exercises in the book honor another tradition of the graphic arts. Old-time editors were also printers, and modern publishers still supervise the printing plant. Students in early graphic arts courses learned to set metal type by hand. A shrewd scholar might have cast off the taint of practice, but I believe that, too, would be unwise. I have included exercises partly because my own best learning has always relied on the applied as well as the abstract. Not only that, but surrendering the practical in favor of pure research or theory also poses grave risks for any discipline involved in making things. Recent failures of space engineering (such as the Hubble telescope fiasco and the Challenger explosion) may be the product of just such a move (Ferguson).

 Cast of Characters

While honoring these traditions, I also raise questions, play devil's advocate, and criticize the values the graphic arts espouse. A critic should probe practical assumptions, argue for more historical depth, and present the contrary opinion that demands rebuttal. These activities require the work of the essayist rather than the encyclopedist. They involve some risk but reward us by encouraging critical thinking about the practices that give the newspaper visual form. Only because the groundwork has been amply laid elsewhere can I take the risk. In these pages, I have written in the first person, telling stories about my own encounters with visual ideas and newspapers. My aim is to acknowledge the particular and individual nature of my observations. As I invite criticism of graphic arts, I hope to make my own prejudices and enthusiasms clear and open to criticism. As I pose alternatives to the standard wisdom and old saws, I see myself less as an authority than as a narrator with a story to tell.

My sons, Matthew, Joel, and Andrew, also make regular appearances in these pages. They have a way of asserting themselves at every stage of my discussion, asking questions and demanding that I make my abstractions concrete. Their reactions to art and the media have made the issues in this book seem urgent. Young people are especially important to the future of newspapers, which have attracted fewer young readers with each recent generation. My sons help to define my position as narrator, and they stand for the next generation, representing the future of the media. They also deserve my earnest thanks for looking after themselves and cooking dinners for me during many long summer days and winter evenings of writing and revision.

Although less apparent, friends and colleagues have also helped to shape the manuscript. Professors John C. Nerone, Ellen Wartella, and D. Charles Whitney read early drafts of several chapters and offered encouragement and advice. E. Everette Dennis gave much-needed support, and the Freedom Forum Media Studies Center, which he directs, provided a one-year research fellowship at Columbia University, where I had the time, the staff assistance, and the kind advice of professors Mercedes de Uriarte, Diana Mutz, and other fellows while writing the first draft. David Rubin, dean of the School of Public Communications, granted a leave of absence from Syracuse University, and the faculty and administrators here made it possible for me to complete revisions. Professors Steve Leuthold and Mark Monmonier and other colleagues here read and offered incisive critiques. I thank them all.

Several chapters were presented at meetings of scholarly societies, and parts of a few have appeared in print along the way. Phi Beta Kappa published Chapter 1 in a slightly shorter form as "The Great American Newspaper" (*American Scholar* 60 [Winter 1991]: 106–12). The first half of Chapter 2 was presented at the 1992 convention of the Association for Education in Journalism and Mass Communication in Montreal. The last half of Chapter 2 was presented at the 1993 Speech Communication Association convention in Miami and published as "The First Exercise, What It Teaches about Photojournalism Practice" (*Journalism Educator* [Summer 1993]: 62–72). Portions of Chapter 4 were presented at the 1992 meetings of the International Visual Literacy Association in Pittsburgh and were included in their proceedings as "The Impact of Legibility Science on the Visual Design of Newspapers" (*Imagery in Science and the Arts*, ed. R. A. Braden, D. G. Beauchamp, and J. Clark-Baca [Blacksburg: IVLA, 1993]: 35–41). The comments of panelists, participants, and editors provided unfailing guidance as I revised the book.

A large number of scholars at other universities also read chapters or the entire manuscript at various stages and wrote lengthy and thoughtful criticisms anonymously: Kay Amert, University of Iowa; Jay Anthony, University of North Carolina at Chapel Hill; Robert Bohle, Virginia Commonwealth University; Lewis Brierly, University of South Carolina; John Center, Temple University; Claude Cookman, Indiana University; I. Wilmer Counts, Indiana University; Robert Craig, University of Ulster at Coleraine; Craig Denton, University of Utah; John Doolittle, American University; Michael Griffin, University of Minnesota; Larry Gross, University of Pennsylvania; Debbie Hankinson, formerly at Syracuse University and now a graphic designer; Susan Herbst, Northwestern University; William Korbus, University of Texas; Vance Kornegay, University of South Carolina; Anne Matthews, Princeton University; Dona Schwartz, University of Minnesota; James Tankard, University of Texas; Birgit L. Wassmuth, University of Missouri–Columbia; Robert Willett, University of Georgia; and Denis Wood, North Carolina State University. I have tried to respond to their suggestions, in detail and in spirit, and hope I have not fallen too short of their expectations.

I owe special thanks to senior editor Cathy Pusateri, who audaciously asked me what book I would like to write, and to editor Jane Lambert, project editor Talvi Laev, and the staff of St. Martin's Press.

The most important character in my story is you, the reader. My college writing teacher told me that if readers are with you at all, they are way ahead of you. Thank you for being twice a reader, of newspapers and of this book—an impressive feat in an age hostile to reading.

Kevin G. Barnhurst
Stoddard, N.H.

CONTENTS

Since my childhood tour of a newspaper's premises, newspapers have transformed themselves into a visual medium, and newspaper design has become a subject of broad interest to readers. To introduce these changes, this book tells stories about myself, my sons, my colleagues, and, most important, about you, the newspaper reader.

Newspapers have infiltrated daily life in myriad ways, yet Americans have little heeded the appearance of the mythological form. Editors and publishers have refashioned that form, in part because of the assumptions of reporters, designers, and researchers. Newspaper redesign accompanied a redefinition of journalism itself, from the coverage of single events to the explanation and analysis of trends. Are these changes for the better? The answer depends on what readers use newspapers for.

CHAPTER 2   UNDERSTANDING PHOTOGRAPHY   21

Are newspaper pictures the crowning achievement of a long progression toward accurately showing reality, or do they show not reality but a stylized version of the truth? Either position can influence ethical decisions journalists make, but the truth falls somewhere between the extremes. General histories of photography often recite a story of technology pushed forward by "great men" who responded to their social milieu. However, pictures also wield ideological power, convey myths, and affect their subjects. Photojournalists have tended to ignore ideology as they invented new ways of thinking about pictures.

EXERCISE: PLAYING PHOTOGRAPHER   45

Amateur snapshots differ from photojournalism because they follow a different set of rules. Editors reaffirm professional rules as they crop and lay out pictures and write captions. The stories that result often reinforce prejudices about people and their roles in society. To protect citizens, photojournalists have set standards of truth, privacy, and community tastes. But whose truth, whose privacy, and whose tastes are served? Amid cultural diversity, photojournalists can use the power of images to break stereotypes and create empathy.

◉

CHAPTER 3   CRITIQUING CHARTS   65

The oldest graphic forms of conveying data were devised by cartographers and engineers. Accounting tables grew out of trade narratives, and graphs out of mathematics. All four types of charts spring from and serve commerce, the military, and technology, establishing social and political power by seeming to reflect a neutral reality. But numbers are invariably rhetorical, containing social judgments that reinforce authority.

EXERCISE: READING NEWSPAPER CHARTS   89

The use of charts in newspapers supposedly makes the facts more functional and striking. Should charts be statistical or persuasive? Journalists disagree, but they have developed standards for completeness and appropriateness, which skirt the larger questions of meaning. Charts may become popular, not for functional but for stylistic reasons, whenever their underlying values become ascendant in society.

CHAPTER 4   INTERPRETING TYPOGRAPHY   109

Writing is one site of the struggle between individual autonomy and social control, and the resulting compromise produces identifiable styles. The pattern of stability and change continued after printing first emerged and is evident in newspapers today. Most newspaper typefaces are Roman in origin and laden with meanings that depend on historical roots as well as recent uses, and newspapers contribute new meanings to the typefaces they employ.

In twentieth-century newspapers, classicists have imitated fine books, while functionalists have pushed for an austere utility. These modernists endorsed efforts to replace, in part, the cultural craft of typography with the universal science of legibility. The resulting move to larger type pushed content off the front pages and tied the newspaper to casual and aging readers. A third school of modern typographic design led newspapers to use type expressively, although their efforts at times amounted to cliché.

CHAPTER 5   EVALUATING LAYOUT   161

Newspapers supposedly took on their traditional appearance because of inattention and accident, but outside forces only partly explain the large format, unusual titles, and vertical makeup of newspapers. Social and cultural forces may also influence newspaper design. The modernists wrote the received history as a polemic against traditional newspaper design, proposing in its place seemingly neutral principles that, in practice, support modernism. One result was an increase in space, which further reduced the content on front pages. To manage increased space, modernists turned to indexes and orderly grids.

Like all newspaper designs, modernism caters to selected tastes and interests by conveying judgments about readers. Recent design trends have turned against the excesses of modernism without necessarily serving a more diverse readership.

CHAPTER 1

SEEING

THE

NEWSPAPER

When he was nine years old, my son for the first time joined

me while I read the Sunday newspaper. He donned his peti-

tioning look — half smile, half squint — and said, "Can I have

the, uh, comics?" I'm territorial when it comes to my news-

paper, but that section, well, it's just a wrapper for the ads

and color supplements. So I handed it over, and he said,

"Thanks," and spread himself out on the rug. A typical

Sunday paper takes me an hour, turning pages from front to back at the dining room table, but when I was finished, he was still poring over the funny papers. Things like "Mary Worth" don't really interest my boy, and so, I wondered, what was he doing? What made him want so badly to use a newspaper that he would wade through comic strips that must be to him incomprehensible?

My own fascination with the newspaper began early. I remember my father, seated in a big armchair, hidden except for his legs and fingertips behind the *Salt Lake Tribune*. My mother read, as I do now, at the table. As a child, I can remember wanting to read the newspaper, too. I began at about my son's age with the comics, first reading "Nancy" and then adding "Beetle Bailey" and others. When I could read them all, I began skipping the ones I didn't care for. Then I would look at the rest of the newspaper, moving from cartoon to cartoon (these were sprinkled around then), and I sometimes discovered amazing little fillers. On the front page, I found "Today's Chuckle," and on the local news page something called "Sam the Sad Cynic Says," in a column by someone named Dan Valentine. Before long, I was reading the whole column. News stories began to catch my eye, and then I was hooked.

Reading the newspaper seemed like a grown-up thing to do. When I started reading the business news, sometime in college, it felt like a rite of passage. Getting through the page was work, but I thought I was old enough, so I stuck with it. Now I browse through those pages, too. I don't know if the way I use the newspaper can be called reading. What once seemed a significant task now seems inconsequential. I hardly pay attention, skimming over the headlines, reading less and less as I get older, or skipping directly to the item or two that I read by habit.

Yet I can't get along without a newspaper. Sometimes in disgust I cancel my local paper, only to subscribe again. My father did this, too, switching to the *Deseret News* and back again. Living in a two-newspaper town, he could have his tantrums without missing a single day's news. While living in the New Hampshire countryside, I would travel ten miles every Sunday through snow, freezing rain, or mud to pick up the *Boston Globe* at the village store — the same trip I would grumble about taking for a gallon of milk. But a newspaper is more than food. It is a ritual, little understood, that I am handing down to my sons. It is a part of my cultural heritage as well as a convenience, a tool for daily living. Even as I read it less I depend on it more, and that makes me curious about the newspaper as an object.

I love the weight of American Sunday newspapers. Pulling them up off the floor is good for the figure.

— *Noel Coward*

Watching my son explore the newspaper made me see it with new eyes, and I didn't like what I saw. Newspapers have changed since I began reading them. Someone has been tinkering. Now, instead of all those real-life events, serendipitous cartoons, clipped opinions, and odd facts, we seem to get fewer and fewer items, all of the less disposable type: literary-style news analysis, fine-art illustrations, arcane criticism, and popular-mechanics charts. In my lifetime, the *New York Times* has slowly metamorphosed from a newspaper of record to a newsmagazine of polite opinion. The elites in my middle American town read it to learn what issues and problems are fashionable. Smaller newspapers follow suit. My local newspaper is not a newspaper of record but of conservative fashion, political as well as social.

The newspaper was once a grubbier, lower, more attractive form. As a product of the machine age, it reached its apex in this century. Picasso, in his collages of 1912–13, identified the role of the newspaper in modern iconography: He cut it up, using news stories as a background for ordinary life, represented by the café table, wine, and music. He thus defined

3

FIGURE 1.1.
The newspaper in modern art. Andy Warhol, *129 Die in Jet! (Plane Crash)*, 1962 (synthetic polymer paint on canvas, 254 x 183 cm, Museum Ludwig, Cologne). Pl. 136 in *Andy Warhol, A Retrospective*, ed. Kynaston McShine (New York: MoMA, 1989) 158.

the newspaper's pervasive role as the typographic texture of this century (Varnedoe and Gopnik). In the 1960s, Andy Warhol's black-and-white paintings of newspaper pages (Figure 1.1) and, in the 1980s, Barbara Kruger's works imitating tabloid typefaces have brought the trend to its contemporary apotheosis. By continuing its present course, the newspaper could become like the foundry type in which our first newspapers were set: a quaint antique, symbolizing a bygone era. As a result, some journalists predict it will metamorphose into another form: The paper won't yellow, the ink won't rub off, and the first edition probably won't be so cheap (Fidler). But before we destroy the popular form, perhaps we should try to find out why the newspaper has changed, how its design affects readers, and what consequences it has for our society.

From Lamp to Light: The Uses of Newsprint

The American newspaper is fascinating in its functions. Before it ends up in the trash, it gets wrapped around rubbish, used to line bird cages or wash windows, rolled up for a weapon against flies, or spread overhead as an umbrella. Children rip it up to make papier-mâché, put it under clay putty and paint boxes, fold it into airplanes and paper hats. It's

FIGURE 1.2. The newspaper as useful object. Vivienne Eisner and Adelle Weiss, *The Newspaper Everything Book* (New York: Dutton, 1975) 70.

a gift wrap, padding for parcels, a drop cloth, tinder, and a wrapper for hot peanuts at the game. Some people even roll logs and make dresses and lamps from it (Figure 1.2). There is something appealing about the pattern and the texture, and also something symbolic.

The newspaper expresses American values—the entrepreneurial zeal of the reporter, interviewing people, being places first. It is objectivity and object, American idealism made material. It is an invention by a culture of inventors, a gadget, a gimcrack, a gizmo, an all-purpose object not unlike the American city — congested, exciting, funny, and just a bit garish. A newspaper is the American persona played up big — a braggart, a schemer, a behind-the-scenes do-gooder, a power broker, a dynamo, a know-it-all. News travels fast, and a newspaper is an artifact of deadlines, hustle, clang and crash, rolls of paper flying through the presses, headlines twice the size of the events shouted rapid-fire from the street corner. The newspaper is American overabundance embodied — an embarrassment of facts, more than anyone could ever digest, a luxury of stories to be mined and picked over, bargain-basement style. It expresses the American love for the compendium, the almanac, the Whitmanesque listing.

The newspaper is an essentially democratic form. Just about everybody can afford one. Because it crosses the barriers of race, money, and status, it is the tributary of universal suffrage. It informs the self-governing citizenry. "Were it left to me to decide whether we should have a government without newspapers, or newspapers without government," said Jefferson, "I should not hesitate a moment to prefer the latter." The newspaper is the fourth estate, a vital check on government, a watchdog for the Republic. On the pages of the newspaper are distilled the misery and misfortune, comedy and catastrophe of national life. Reading news is a civic duty taught in American schools. Citizens assert more proprietary interest in their local newspaper than they do in any mere business. We call it "our newspaper," and we chastise it for any lapse in completeness or accuracy because it is the tangible record of our community life. But it records more than that. The local newspaper chronicles important events from the lives of acquaintances, neighbors, friends—lives like our own. Personal experience day by day is played against a backdrop of news. We remember our own lives by the texture of the news of the day. And once in a while our own lives become news.

What is to prevent a daily newspaper from being made the greatest organ of social life?

— *James Gordon Bennett, Sr.*

My family has appeared in the newspaper spotlight only a few times. Once was when my sister fell from our apartment window. She was only two or three years old, trying to reach a doll propped on the sill. She fell two-and-a-half stories to the sidewalk below and survived only because she landed on the doll. That was a news story. I know about it (this was before I was born) because the family has two relics of the event. One is my sister's bent little finger, which was the only thing broken in the fall; the other is a newspaper clipping ("Doll Breaks Drop"). In some envelope or bureau or trunk, American families save the clippings about our births and weddings and blue ribbons won. A relative once showed me the front-page story about my mom. She was identified as a mother of six. The reporter had tried to reconstruct the last moments of her life, before she fell from Ensign Peak near Salt Lake City ("Fall Injury Fatal"). The paper was yellowed and worn. It felt strangely thick and brittle. I held it only for a moment before folding it back into its place between the pages of a book. These scraps of newsprint bearing the traces of our lives are somehow beyond price.

No printed medium has as much room for ordinary people as a newspaper does. Books are for the renowned, magazines for the celebrity. As a child, I was taught to respect books, not to write in them, fold them, or tear them, but to handle them with care, to use a bookmark, a book bag, and to make a brown-paper cover. My family treasured any magazines that came into the house. Copies of *National Geographic* were displayed on the coffee table, arrayed in the shape of a fan. A far cry from the stately book or chic magazine, the newspaper is jury-rigged, a Rube Goldberg form — big, fat, and dirty, like old American industry. The ink comes off on your fingers and clothes. The paper smells of dust and makes you sneeze. Inelegant and ephemeral, the newspaper is least among forms. But it bears examination because it has entered the American mythology, an image enshrined by a process Roland Barthes called signification.

Elements and Attributes of the Form

Americans pay scant attention to the visible form of things. Such considerations are thought to be mere window dressing for the substance that lies in words and actions. Aesthetic concerns, devoid of practical value, are relegated to kindergarten, where art is a form of play. In school, Americans study words, and our visual knowledge remains as we acquired it in childhood. Visually uneducated, we find it difficult to appraise the form rather than the content of the news. If we could again see a newspaper as a child does before learning to read, we would be aware of it as an object. Instead of events and ideas, the page would be the sum of its musty smell and taste, the crackling sounds it makes, and its significant link to our parents. Somewhere in our earliest memories, we retain this sensual and emotional tie to the newspaper form.

The visual appearance of the page — the blacks and whites in different textures and shades of gray, forming a multitude of shapes in many sizes — still resonates with meaning, even if it is inarticulate (Barnhurst). When we see a horizontal shape, even as a small child, we can make sense of it by drawing on our experience with flat things in the environment. The horizon, building foundations, and our own position in sleep seem tranquil. We can associate anything vertical with standing erect and with the precarious images of cliffs and skyscrapers.

In a newspaper, short lines of type get stacked into vertical shapes. The same text in long lines will make a low horizontal shape. Research suggests that horizontal blocks of text seem comfortable (Middlestadt); vertical columns create a hostile environment for reading. But at either extreme the lines will cause discomfort: too short, and you're jumping constantly from word to word and struggling with hyphenations; too long, and you get lost going from one line down to the next (see Chapter 4 on typography).

All the graphic attributes of the text and headlines — how large the type is, the amount of space between the lines — can be varied to extremes or kept neutral. Headlines with bold, condensed, italic type made entirely of capital letters seem active; headlines with lighter weights and lowercase letters seem calmer. Laying out a newspaper page involves dozens of

> *J*ournalism consists in buying white paper at two cents a pound and selling it at ten cents a pound.
>
> — *Charles A. Dana*

decisions about the size and shape not only of text but of pictures and other elements (see Chapter 5 on layout). Each decision pushes the image toward the calm or energetic extremes, or nearer the neutral ground.

Any newspaper we read conveys its personality through the accumulation of these visual cues. We assume that it is the writing that makes the difference, but that is only partly true. When we see the same wire story laid out differently in, say, the *Washington Post* and the *New York Post*, we draw different conclusions about the quality, clarity, and authority of the

FIGURE 1.3. The archetypal newspaper. *New York World Telegram* 18 Feb. 1932. Rpt. in *America's Front Page News*, ed. Michael C. Emery, R. Smith Schuneman, and Edwin Emery (New York: Doubleday, 1970) 130.

writing. No matter how strenuously we may deny it, the form of the news matters. It elicits meanings from our personal experience. It gives substance to a ritual of daily living and weaves our individual lives into the fabric of American culture.

The form of the newspaper developed slowly, beginning late in the eighteenth century, as American journalists adapted the newspaper from its European antecedents. The process was an accretion, like the building of a coral reef. By the 1930s, enough structural remains of the attitudes, values, and beliefs of publishers and journalists had accumulated that the newspaper became the embodiment of an American myth, its contours clearly defined (Figure 1.3). The form was a naïve expression of the culture, its philosophy democratic and idealistic, its personality busy, crowded, and complicated. It was a seat-of-the-pants product of people and machinery driven to the limits to put out all the news first, however crude the form. Strong, a little pushy or brazen, the newspaper embodied perfectly the urgent and combative quality of the news. This American mythology is stored in cultural memory as an image, and it probably bears more resemblance to the *Daily Planet* than to any real newspaper.

*N*ews has
a short
shelf life.

— *Harford Thomas*

If you were to invent a form that expressed the whole brash hubbub of daily news, you would probably recreate the mythological American newspaper, and it would probably look something like this: The text typography would be as small as possible, pushing right to the limits of intelligibility (and beyond what some could read without a magnifying glass). You would make the columns narrow, say four or five words wide (about one alphabet). Text columns would be very vertical, as vertical as you could get them. For headlines, you would choose typography that again pushes the reader to the limits, would make them bold, condensed, all capital letters—

all the things that emphasize the vertical aspects of the letterform. You would use a typeface that is crude and dense, one that would withstand the pounding of thousands of impressions of metal on paper. You would use italic type. Legibility research (see Chapter 4) shows that all these things present difficulties for the reader; but then, so does news. Instead of arranging the elements neatly in boxes, you would scatter them and build up irregular shapes, so that stories, especially major ones, would have a jagged silhouette. You wouldn't leave any space but would crowd everything in, and you would develop a complex system that would create layering, so that at any distance, new items would become apparent. You would cram in as many tiny items as you could. Of course you would use pictures that were equally active: people at war, riots, or at the very least, felons being led from court. You would play them as large as the dense packing of the page would permit, but never so large that they did not seem detailed, and you would squeeze in mug shots to exaggerate the difference of scale.

I am not talking here about any single styling detail that newspaper editors like to debate, such as whether to use ruled lines between the columns or a specific typeface like Bodoni. The newspaper has taken a thousand individual styles within the larger parameters of this mythological form. What is significant is not the particulars of dress but the overall pattern, which reveals our assumptions about the role of the newspaper in culture and its use by common people.

 ismantling the Mythological Newspaper

Reporters and editors nowadays believe that their stories get read much as a book gets read, only quicker. For that purpose, a busy, crowded, complicated newspaper will not do. What is needed, it is felt, is clarity and simplicity, so that the ideas can flow unhindered by the setting. Besides their aim to inform the reader, editors will also admit other purposes: to entertain, warn, persuade, enlighten, and so on. These uses are no different from those of a book and are best served by the clear, simple appearance of a book page. When editors hire researchers to study the best typography, they convey these purposes. And researchers bring their own set of assumptions. Typographic research has traditionally focused on the problems of legibility (whether letterforms can be easily identified) and readability (whether words can be comfortably understood). The researcher typically measures the speed of reading and the comprehension, two activities enhanced by a neutral typographic form, such as that found in books.

🔲 Designers and artists contribute yet another set of assumptions about newspaper design, most of them based on aesthetics. They want the newspaper page to achieve a measure of unity, balance, contrast, rhythm, and proportion. This vocabulary of form, attributed to classical philosophy (see Chapter 5), suggests a marketing strategy: Make the page pleasing to the eye, and thus entice the reader to sample the editorial product. Artists tend to admire the painting as a form, designers the book. In art school, the newspaper doesn't rate.

Now these assumptions of writers, artists, and researchers would never get you to the mythological newspaper form I described earlier. The typography of the text, if you tested it on any group, would not score well on any of the measures of legibility. The researcher would say, make the columns wider, make the type larger, use a face that is less crude so that the form of each letter is more legible. The researcher could

$\mathcal{N}$ewspapers are the schoolmasters of the common people. That endless book, the newspaper, is our national glory.

— *Henry Ward Beecher*

FIGURE 1.4.
The high
modern news-
paper.
*Midland
Reporter-
Telegram*
[Texas] 4 Feb.
1978: 1. Rpt.
in García 36.

prove that type in all capital letters is hard to read, that bold type is hard to read. Indented, italic, and centered headlines would not test nearly as well as any of the less tortured forms. The researcher would say, get rid of the boldface, make the headline "down style" (lowercase except for the initial capital letter) in roman type of a reasonable size, and don't make the lines either horribly long or short. Keep everything in the neutral zone.

The graphic artist would hate *everything* about the typography and would strongly support the researcher — but would add a few more suggestions. She would dislike the irregular shapes and would want those jagged forms removed. She would want all the little items, spread haphazardly on the page, to be grouped together and given a home. Order and logic would require that. There's just too much going on here, she would say, and besides, with this new, larger type on wider, more horizontal columns, you've got to get rid of all this junk, clean it out. Then it will look accessible, inviting. So the designer, along with the researcher, pushes, and the poor editor, like any naïve artist, yields. After all, the editor thinks, reporters want their stories longer and photographers want their pictures bigger. And, anyhow, these complicated pages are hard to lay out!

What these assumptions of writers, artists, and researchers have done, bit by bit, is dismantle the newspaper's native, expressive, mythological form. Publishers first began to hire typography and marketing experts in the 1930s and graphic designers in the 1960s. By the 1970s, the newspaper began to resemble something else entirely. It looked like a book, or a magazine, or a poster — anything but a newspaper. By 1980, Mario García, a leading newspaper consultant, admired the Midland, Texas, newspaper (Figure 1.4) for being "clean, easy-to-read," for its "large photos, and an almost totally horizontal format for its front page. The nameplate . . . has been surrounded with white space. . . . Few stories are played up on page one, but they are packaged to provide comfortable reading. The headlines show little size variation. . . . This type of front page is easy to design and easy to look at" (36).

The New Long Journalism

The content of the newspaper changed as well. Stories were longer, and there were fewer of them. Where once a reporter had written at least a half-dozen stories in a day, now he wrote one or part of one. Instead of three stories written about three different fires in the city, an editor would run only the biggest or combine the information from all three into one story built around a similarity, a unifying element or theme. One of the fires might be described as an example, representing all the fires of that sort, or the story might focus on any of a number of fire-related issues or trends. Somewhere along the line, editors, perceiving a need to differentiate a newspaper from a television set, hit upon the length of the story as print journalism's principal distinction. Stories, they discovered, could be made longer by spinning out the facts into a web of interpretations, historical as well as topical. And that is what journalists did.

The new long journalism removed a critical, structural

support from the traditional, mythological newspaper. Individual lives, in long journalism, came to be treated as examples of larger problems, and the newspaper became distanced from the individual citizen. But news that is less particular is more frustrating than cathartic. Fires end, but issues are never resolved. In the long journalism, the house across town didn't burn; instead, society confronted a chronic wiring problem in its aging stock of housing.

This shift from reporting single events to creating news roundups and analyses has contributed to the widespread perception of the last thirty years that we have more problems and that they have become more intractable (Rosenblatt). It has also fed the public sense that editors report only bad news. Although it is not so much the negative events as it is the negative *meanings* that readers find oppressive, their objections have spurred the effort to make the news at least *look* better. But cleaning up the form has only exacerbated the problem. Alternative tabloids designed in the 1970s commonly had a single story on page 1. Even the supermarket tabloids did not remain immune. The *National Enquirer* and the *Star* redesigned their front pages, and weird stories about aliens and deformed babies began to appear in neat little boxes reproduced in crisp color, an utter contradiction between form and content. Readers are not fooled by these beautification projects; their response in focus-group research (García) has been to say that the world is not so neat and pretty.

> *It's not the world that's got so much worse but the news coverage that's got so much better.*
> — G. K. Chesterton

In the 1980s, some newspapers, influenced by *USA Today*, put more charts and graphs on the page, adopted color, and so on. These changes made newspapers resemble television. Editors revile *USA Today* because it joined the competition. Even its vending machines look like television sets. Not only its form but also its contents break with the newspaper of mythology. Despite the brevity, its reporting places even greater distance between individuals and the news by subsuming them into the mass (see Chapter 3 on charts), where they participate in trends that begin with the phrase "We're becoming more. . . ."

Something significant has happened to newspapers, and it has principally to do with the scale of things. The page itself has gotten smaller as the price of newsprint has gone up, and, because of the assumptions of editors and designers, the things on the page have gotten larger and fewer (Barnhurst and Nerone). You could probably fit the contents of two or three contemporary front pages onto one front page of the *Daily Planet*.

The size of things in a newspaper expresses the fundamental definition of what is news. How "big" a story is, whether it gets on the front page or into the newspaper at all, has come to depend on its level of abstraction, on the secondary meaning that a reporter or editor can assign it. This journalism flies in the face of the broadly accepted sense of the term. To characterize any writing as journalistic places it within a tradition bounded by the "direct presentation of facts or description of events without an attempt at interpretation," to quote Merriam-Webster. Covering events in the lives of common people, once the heart of reporting, has become a drudgery to be avoided in the new long journalism. A typical undergraduate journalism assignment is to analyze the meaning of an event, to do what professors call "making sense" of the news. The typical cub reporter wants to be a columnist, to write opinion and commentary, which is believed, rightly or wrongly, to provide the ultimate freedom from reporting ordinary news events. Reporters

> *What is a newspaper but a sponge or invention for oblivion.*
> — *Ralph Waldo Emerson*

16

interview other reporters, asking for news analysis, or they all go on radio or television to present their differing points of view. With so much going on in the world, journalists argue, readers need packaged explanations. The facts alone lack meaning. All of these changes are to the good, if newspaper editors and designers are right in their assumptions about how we use the newspaper. Are they right? I don't think so.

The Uses of the Newspaper

What is the function of a newspaper? Do people read it the way they read a book or a magazine? I doubt that any well-conceived study would show that they do. The newspaper's role in culture has little to do with reading and nothing to do with beauty (Barnhurst and Wartella). It is not meant to be read or admired at all but to be confronted, like the enemy. We attack it and tear it apart, write on it, and cut it up, doing socially acceptable vandalism without guilt. No other medium allows that freedom.

My father was a devoted newspaper reader. When he came home from the meat market, tired and short-tempered, he looked for the paper. If it arrived late, he paced around the house, went out to look in the bushes again, and muttered and swore until the paper landed with a whop on the front step. Then he would settle into his chair and roll back the rubber band before snapping the paper flat, just so. I never saw my father read a book, but he read the paper, silently for the most part. He never exclaimed at it or said, "Listen to this," as my mother sometimes did. But he read it every day, and we children would tiptoe around or go outside to wait.

I don't know what my father did when he was reading, but I don't think his purpose was to find information, to be entertained, to become a better citizen, or to pass the time. I believe he used the newspaper in another way. For twenty minutes perhaps, he glanced at stories about an Israeli military action in the Suez, a racial incident in the South, or one of Stevenson's attacks on Eisenhower, the part-time president. He might even have read a few paragraphs about traffic or hunting accidents, bad weather in Idaho, or the boy-and-girl-gang fights on Salt Lake's west side. His own life, by comparison, must have seemed easy, or at least the news put his problems into perspective. Looking at the newspaper, he knew just how bad it could get. The tightly packed troubles on those pages acted as a catharsis. After reading, he would roll the paper up and whack the ottoman with it, feigning anger. And then he would smile.

"People don't actually read newspapers," wrote Marshall McLuhan. "They get into them every morning like a hot bath." Research indicates that ordinary people do not read newspapers. They look at them (García and Stark). They scan the headlines, read a few lines here, a paragraph there. The story they read in its entirety is the exception. They come away with "Nun Dies in Fire; Children Saved" and little more. Most of the news we don't need to know about. Reading a news story is like coming upon an accident: We don't want to see it but can't stop ourselves from looking. A glance is enough. We don't want beautiful news pages. We want to marvel, yes, but also to resist. In one sense, the newspaper exerts social control by showing that crime never pays, by exposing corruption and greed. We ordinary readers can come away feeling justified and maybe a touch self-righteous, our prejudices and pretensions affirmed. Reading the newspaper can also assert individual freedom to pick and choose, ignoring what doesn't appeal to us. The newspaper is then an artifact of our birthright of freedom. Finally, the newspaper provides a means of self-control. In a society of unbridled expectations, a daily dose of news can make our burden seem lighter. It is a damper on our discontent.

> *A* good newspaper is a nation talking to itself.
>
> — *Arthur Miller*

It is typical of Americans to take our purgative in private and to view the act pragmatically and egotistically. We use the news like a mouthwash, the newspaper like an appliance. The value we put on the form cannot be measured in Pulitzers or design awards but by how assiduously we rip the thing apart, how many uses we invent for it, and how many items we clip and mail or keep taped to the fridge so long that they crumble. Anyone who has packed up to move has found pages from an old newspaper lining the bottom of the trunk or dresser drawer. The discovery is poignant. We pause to remember and to wish the paper were more durable before we throw it away. A newspaper is a symbol of memory. It is ubiquitous in literature and film, where it prods characters to both recollection and action. We treat our life lightly each day it arrives, we say we want it to instruct and improve us, but we are inattentive and we use it up for other things. Memories we want to preserve and cherish, but they are made of newsprint.

CHAPTER 2

My first camera was miniature, the size and shape of a pack-

age of squarish lozenges. It was made of black plastic and used

𝒰NDERSTANDING

16-mm film. I had saved money for months to send off to a

PHOTOGRAPHY

mail-order house that had all sorts of items meant to appeal to

eleven-year-olds. The tiny square advertisement in the catalog

claimed the camera was small enough for a spy. Spies were

still admired in the early 1960s, but I didn't care about that. I wanted a camera, and this one I could afford. When my eleven-year-old son got his first camera, the world had changed. Disposable 35-mm cameras sold in the drugstore for less than two weeks' allowance. Film was not cheap, but developing cost next to nothing by mail. Pictures were ubiquitous, and owning a camera did not have the significance it had once had for eleven-year-olds. The change in just one generation—not merely in the technology but in what owning a camera means—suggests that the history of picture making is anything but stable. The pictures made for newspapers absorb the values of their times, and the first step to understanding photojournalism is to study the histories of pictures. The first half of this chapter introduces those stories.

When my first camera arrived in the mail, I discovered it was even smaller and less sturdy than it had looked in the catalog. Developing and reordering film turned out to be expensive. So I took care of the camera to make it last. I hoarded film, shooting pictures only to capture important events or to record the places and people important in my life. I lost the camera long ago, but I still have the pictures—conventional poses of the family in front of the car, scenes from my trip to Idaho. These are stored in a trunk along with other pictures—postcards and newspaper clippings showing places I went and people I knew. For me, pictures have always been mementos, an extension of my private history.

When my son got his camera, he proceeded to take pictures of just about anything—peculiar shots of a building he made of blocks, blurry close-ups of an outscale Transformer toy called Repugnes (Figure 2.1), his bedroom (mostly the ceiling) from an odd, low angle. He snapped no portraits of loved ones, no scenes of significant moments, no records of landmarks. Family members appeared as blurs in the background or running off the edges of the prints. At first I thought my son lacked technical instruction, that he was bumping the camera and releasing the shutter by mistake. But I was wrong. His pictures were made just as deliberately as any I have stored in the

FIGURE 2.1.
Snapshot of
toy. Andrew
Barnhurst,
1989.

attic. Still, I found myself urging him to conform to the conventions, to take the snapshots I had taken. This he resisted. On a trip to Washington, D.C., he didn't want me posing in front of the Capitol. The only pictures like that on the roll were the ones I took of him. Instead, he made pictures from inside the car, at any angle, with the Washington Monument tilted and obscured by the windshield reflections and auto body parts. It is a record as different as anything I can imagine.

Each generation revises the conventions of picture making. As individuals take pictures, they not only express their individual perspectives but also contribute a view of the times. My son's pictures belong to the decade of MTV and *USA Today*. Contemporary snapshots, videos, and photojournalism reveal assumptions about the uses and meanings of pictures in society. My son's generation clearly has less use for conventional news pictures than previous generations have had. Looking at what photojournalists do — the conventions they follow — may suggest ways that pictures can evolve. The second half of this chapter introduces the issues involved in the practice of photojournalism.

The Traditional History of Pictures

The significance of photographs in the newspaper derives in part from the larger purposes and meanings of pictures in civilization. Historians have worked under several grand narrative schemes that infuse meaning into their telling of the story of pictures. One version of the history of picture making, from the caves to the present, retells an unflagging movement toward the ever more accurate reflection of the real world. This traditional narrative gets expressed implicitly in many histories of the arts and has also been critiqued explicitly (e.g., Mitchell; Ivins; Panofsky, *Meaning*). Many histories of photography (e.g., Eder; Gernsheim and Gernsheim) and summary accounts of photojournalism history (e.g., Hoy; Geraci) also build on the tacit assumption that centuries of technological progress have driven civilization ever closer to reproducing reality more accurately.

In the traditional history, progress from the caves to the Romans established the ideal: A good picture shows how things look. The Roman scholar Pliny illustrated this ideal in retelling the story of a competition between painters (Hardin). The winner painted only a curtain, but one so realistic that his opponent asked him to draw it back to uncover the painting beneath (compare Figure 2.2). Pliny's story illustrates how pictures not only mimicked reality but also served the storyteller. The classical ideal defined pictures as a means of retelling events, which could be read from the depicted scene (Griffin). In the traditional histories, this classical ideal has guided the material progress of pictures ever since. Each succeeding generation contributed techniques, so that picture making slowly came to approximate the real.

In the traditional version, two great advances occurred. The first was the development of linear perspective in the Renaissance (Panofsky, *Perspective*). Artists discovered a geometric structure underlying vision and applied it systematical-

FIGURE 2.2. Curtains and window comment on illusion and reality in painting. René Magritte, *La condition humaine*, 1933 (oil on canvas, 100 x 81 cm). Pl. 109 in *Rétrospective Magritte* (Houston: Menil Foundation, 1978).

ly to make their pictures seem more real. The humanist Leon Battista Alberti described the technique in detail in the fifteenth century. Many other material advances enhanced picture making. New pigments and glazes rendered colors more accurately. The method called chiaroscuro reproduced the effects of light and shadow. Together these techniques made oil paintings the principal images of the emerging modern world (Berger).

At the same time, progress in science is thought to have made observation more precise (Crary). Galileo's telescope plays a role, but the device central in the traditional history is the *camera obscura*, a dark room with a hole in one wall, through which the light from outside could enter to cast an image on the opposite wall. Lenses sharpened and focused the image, and further refinements made the camera obscura a portable aid to observing as well as painting. Science made other enhancements to the accuracy of observation, results of the study of optics and the eye and also of Newton's contribution to the physics of light.

The progress of picture making supposedly culminated in the nineteenth century with the second great advance: the discovery of photographic processes. The photograph, in this version of history, is the crowning fulfillment of the classical ideal. Ingenious inventors harnessed the natural effect of light on certain chemicals in order to record the visible world. The camera made all the realistic effects of painting seem artificial by comparison (Newhall, "Daguerreotype"). The machine took an impression of the world, written by the sun itself, and recorded almost any object in its "real" state. Deprived of a central role in representing the world, painting veered off into abstraction and expressionism, leaving photography as the principal method of rendering images in the twentieth century (Schwarz).

Critical Histories of Pictures

This traditional history, recounted only in its broadest outlines here, has several weaknesses. The most glaring is the notion that pictures reproduce reality. Numerous scholars dismiss the idea that pictures have rendered nature ever more truthfully, suggesting that each generation has instead imposed a new set of conventions (e.g., Snyder; Crary), or what the sociologist Arnold Hauser calls "a new fictitious equivalent of truth to nature" (405). A related weakness is the notion that painting and photography rival each other in the task of showing the real. Several historians question this belief (e.g., Coke; Galassi), arguing that painting and photography interrelate in complex ways that have, as the German literary critic Walter Benjamin argues, transformed the ways in which people perceive. From these broad critiques, other versions of history have emerged. Instead of a tale of progress toward truth, newer critics recount the history of picture making as ideological, the story of an idea that became dominant.

The dominant idea that most of these critical histories assail is the following metaphor: What humans see with their eyes is a picture of the world. This belief that human sight is cameralike has become so deeply ingrained in Western culture that alternatives seem unimaginable. Eyesight merely appears to supply pictures of the real world. Pictures, including paintings, etchings, drawings, photographs, and the like, often resemble the images before our eyes. But a picture has many qualities these images do not — for example, a flat surface with defined objects, an orientation to vertical and horizontal axes, a defining frame, an illusion of volume, and a geometric system suggesting spatial depth. The critical historians follow Nelson Goodman and E. H. Gombrich in arguing that, far from reproducing the effects of human eyesight, pictures substitute a range of artificial conventions that society accepts as natural.

The pictures that the traditional history would label early, primitive, or naïve steps toward reality become, in the critical histories, alternatives to the classical picture metaphor. Instead of arranging objects vertically and horizontally, Paleolithic art overlaid many competing orientations. Much of the art of the Middle East eventually rejected depiction of objects in favor of ornamental decoration. A frame is a theatrical effect, like the proscenium of a Greek stage, which segregates objects into a separate space and suggests both storytelling and dramatic illusion. Round, arched, and oval frames were more common when pictures decorated the surfaces of walls and furniture. Within the frame, Egyptian drawing had little or no illusionary volume, in contrast with Egyptian sculpture. Finally, instead of using geometry to create the illusion of distance, Eastern and European artists of the Middle Ages used scale or size to suggest the importance of objects.

None of these views was any closer to natural vision than another. But among the alternatives, the critics observe, the defined object on a rigid axis became the effect accepted as the norm in the West. Artists combined this effect with tonal value within a frame, usually rectangular, to create systems of perspective, in which large objects near the bottom were defined as closer, and small, faint objects rendered high in the frame were considered further away. Numerous examples show how the system worked out its contradictions, such as the fact that not everything small and pale is necessarily far away.

The critical histories see the development of the system of perspective from the caves to the early modern period less as a result of technical improvements than as evidence of the spread of an ideal. The picture metaphor of the classical era set the direction of these changes and drove the transformation of technique. In the critical view, the Renaissance not only advanced the classical ideal but also defined the metaphor. Alberti's contribution was to restate the elements of the picture metaphor so that they seemed natural and were easily grasped. Thinking of a picture as a view through a window, as Alberti proposed, seemed obvious, while obscuring the contrivances of the orientation, frame, objects, and space. A window, after all, is itself artificial, not a naturally occurring phenomenon.

What the Renaissance did, the critical historians suggest, was define spatial relations geometrically. Linear perspective employs all the elements of visual design — positions and straight lines, shapes or objects arrayed in diagonal directions, space defined by receding scale, tonal value, and color—to turn a curved or contradictory world into a rational, linear ideal. The transformation requires a vision alien to human eyesight. In its place, painters created a version of things seen by a Cyclops, whose eye remains immobile, recording uniformly the details before it as it peers from a box that sharply and geometrically demarcates the edges of its field of vision (Barnhurst).

The system is complex to learn and to execute, and the difficulties are thought to have motivated a search for mechanical aids to drawing. Techniques such as drawing on grid paper or using an observation point and a frame (as Dürer's often-reproduced woodcuts illustrate) joined many other tools to help artists master the daunting task of remaking the world geometrically. Linear perspective, as the operating system for the picture metaphor, had its greatest impact on the technology of lenses. The verticals and horizontals, the frame, the straight diagonals and elliptical foreshortening of curves, and the uniform detail ruled the development of optical instruments, leading eventually to the photographic camera.

Critics disagree over the precise roles of these devices in history. Joel Snyder, like most historians of photography, considers the camera obscura a direct ancestor of the photographic camera. Jonathan Crary, however, argues that the rationalist model embodied in the camera obscura was replaced in the 1820s. Crary suggests that the early nineteenth century placed vision not within a detached observer witnessing objects in the physical world, but rather within a subjective observer who encountered images detached from their origins in the physical world. This shift in ideas predated by a century the abstract and expressionist movements in art, which resulted not so much from the rivalry between painting and photography as

> *All* I know
> is what I see
> in the papers.
>
> — *Will Rogers*

from the ways in which perception had changed. Whatever their disagreements, most critics now conclude that evolving techniques did not increasingly approximate the real world.

Critical histories propose that the picture metaphor not only influenced the common perception of vision but also changed the role of pictures in society. Some historians have argued that by redefining vision to conform to the classical ideal, the thinkers of the early modern period transformed pictures from fixtures of worship and veneration. While retaining their value as a testimony of wealth and eminence, pictures also became commodities of trade and commerce (Mukerji). In the traditional view, pictures provide windows on the world. In the critical view, they become conventional consumer items that reveal as much about ideals as about reality.

What Picture Theories Mean to Journalists

The larger argument between the traditional and critical histories has consequences for how readers and journalists use and understand pictures. If you believe with the traditionalists that pictures show the real world, you are likely to applaud the photojournalists who say, "Shoot first, ask questions later." You are also more likely to admit the possibility that advertising pictures depict some corner of reality, no matter how remote. If you adopt the critical position, you might condemn the photojournalist for any pretense of playing fly-on-the-wall and merely reflecting reality. Instead, you would argue that photojournalists actively promote a certain version of reality. You might also be extremely skeptical of advertisers who try to create an image of reality that includes their products, services, or worldviews.

As in most such arguments, each side possesses some portion of the truth. The resemblance of many pictures to the real world can hardly be denied. Perceptual psychology buttresses the link between pictures and vision. While arguing strenuously against confusing pictures and retinal images with reality, the psychologist James J. Gibson maintained that the act of recognizing pictures corresponds to the experience of seeing things in the physical world. Subsequently, the late perceptual psychologist David Marr described the operations of perception: outlining shapes, adding depth, and then identifying objects. Experiments in a variety of cultures and settings uninfluenced by picture conventions tend to confirm that the ability to recognize pictures springs from experience in the real world, not from social learning (Messaris).

However, even given a fundamental correlation between pictures and reality, perceptual psychology cannot refute the role of convention. It is possible to argue that even the basic recognizing operations are influenced or controlled by what David Novitz in philosophy calls "umbrella" conventions. But if Gibson and Marr are right in saying that making and recognizing pictures depends on experience with vision, there is still room for conventions. The eye and brain, which perceive stick figures as readily as photographs, leave the bulk of the picture — that is, most of the surface — under artistic and social control. In every detail beyond whatever is essential to recognition, the powerful effects of social attitudes and norms are felt. Like traditional reality, critical conventionality can hardly be denied.

So where does this leave the newspaper practitioner and reader? A moderate position might allow for the reality behind news (and advertising) pictures, acknowledge the good or neutral intentions of their creators, but engage in a careful study of the ideas, latent and manifest, they espouse. Visually aware editors and readers need not let go of concrete reality to enter into thoroughgoing critical analyses of photography.

Histories of Photography

Within the larger framework of picture making, the history of photography is but a recent phase, usually thought to have begun in 1839. The earliest histories of photography concentrated almost entirely on the inventions of science and technology (e.g., Eder; Stenger). The technical details in these histories shared a spotlight with stories about inventors, who were presented as objects of national pride (Gernsheim and Gernsheim). As photographs began appearing in galleries and museums, aesthetic versions of photography's history emerged (e.g., Newhall, *History;* Szarkowski, *Photographer's;* Bayer). Several authors also sought to broaden the scope of the history to include the social context in which photography flourished (e.g., Taft; Freund; Braive).

From a purely technical viewpoint, the history of photography is a story of material progress in the sciences of physics and chemistry and in the mechanics of camera building. Like the traditional history of pictures, this technical history recounts a series of discoveries stretching back to the Greeks and accelerating with the many "firsts" in the eighteenth and nineteenth centuries. This strain of thinking dominates the early, important history written by the German chemist Josef Maria Eder. His account set the pattern, unbroken in most subsequent histories, of reciting the events in scientific and engineering progress. The technical assumed a central role early on, not only because scientists wrote the histories but also because science acquired immense authority in contemporary culture.

Another strain in these histories is authorial, concerned with giving credit to individual philosophers, scientists, and tinkerers who contributed to technical progress and also with sorting out their competing claims. The process exposes a lingering nationalism, Eder championing the German role, the French authors proclaiming their country's preeminence, the British chafing against being ignored, and the Americans asserting their technical superiority. These historians honor the authentic pioneers by preserving them in biographies of triumph and tragedy. Eder enshrines Johan Heinrich Schulze for discovering photographic chemistry in 1727, Nicéphore

Niepce for inventing camera photography in 1822, Louis Daguerre for perfecting the process from 1829 to 1837, William Fox Talbot for inventing negative and paper-positive photography in 1839, and so forth. The emphasis on individual accomplishments, in the "great men" tradition of history, extends to most writing on photography.

A further strain in photographic history is aesthetic, a story of the pictures that won acclaim as works of art. The aesthetic history also tracks the progress of the profession into the ranks of the fine arts. The original work of aesthetic photo history springs not from laboratories but from art museums. A classic among these histories is by Beaumont Newhall, then librarian at the Museum of Modern Art, whose catalog for a 1937 exhibition (*Photography*) subsequently grew into a full-length art history of photography. Newhall begins with the camera obscura and returns continually to the established technical history of photography. Much of his history concerns itself with issues of authorship. He proposes that photography's inventors worked from artistic urges and laments that individual daguerreotypists cannot be identified.

> *What you see is news, what you know is background, and what you feel is opinion.*
>
> — *Lester Markel*

🕲 The central issue in Newhall's history — the relationship between photography and art — is addressed in most aesthetic histories. Besides asserting the equality of photography with the other graphic arts, aesthetic histories suggest standards of criticism. Newhall based his selections on optical detail and chemical tonal value, both used by the photographer to produce pleasure. Aesthetic histories describe how artists express personal emotion through composition, within the limitations of the photographic medium. Artists who most often emerge from these histories include Eugene Atget, Gaspard Félix Tournachon (Nadar), and the nineteenth-century portraitists; Alfred

Stieglitz and his associates in the Photo-Secession; and Walker Evans, Paul Strand, and other artist-advocates of "straight" photography.

Yet another strain in the history is social, a concern with the conditions and events in society contemporary with the discoveries and the pioneers who made them. Although Eder's later editions cite the emergence of photography societies, and Newhall describes conditions such as the popular demand for pictures, the groundbreaking social history is by Robert Taft. His book takes an American view, crediting Mathew B. Brady and his assistants with inventing the idea of pictorial history during the Civil War and William H. Jackson, among others, with recording the physical landscapes of the frontier expansion. Like Taft, social historians explore the ways people used photography, in family albums and parlor stereoscopes. Michel Braive, for example, studies travelers and sitters for photographic portraits.

These histories also point out the roles of social institutions that use photography, such as the mass media. Gisele Freund, for example, has explored the ways society uses photography in the arts and in politics. Documentary and press photography play a larger role in these than in technical or aesthetic histories. They begin with Roger Fenton's pictures of the Crimean War and continue with the turn-of-the-century reform crusades of Jacob Riis and Lewis Hine.

Although the social and aesthetic versions of history came as a reaction against the first, technical histories, taken as a whole, the story of photography may seem fairly complete. The actors and props are there: a photograph, a camera, a photographer, and a social context. Technical histories explain the camera, aesthetic histories the photograph, both describe the photographer, and social histories describe contemporary conditions. Historians working through the middle of the twentieth century seem to have described the entire scene quite thoroughly.

Critical Histories of Photography

However, other important elements in the photographic scene are left out, such as the values and myths of the cultures in which the scenes take place, the status of the photograph as information, the political and economic power of the players, and the ethics of the exchanges among them. The most powerful evidence of these oversights is that not much attention is paid to the people sitting in front of the camera. During the 1970s, the essays of Susan Sontag and Allan Sekula and the BBC series Ways of Seeing, hosted by John Berger, challenged the comfortable assumptions that made photographic history seem complete. These critics had been preceded—by Marshall McLuhan in raising social issues during the 1960s and, even earlier, by Walter Benjamin—in questioning the emphasis on techniques, authorship, aesthetics, and social description.

In response to these critics, another strain of photographic history has emerged (e.g., Bolton; Guimond; Schloss). Critical histories question the meaning of photography in culture as well as the assumptions of the other strains of its history. Although still concerned with the authorial lineage of famous photographers and the status of pictures within art, Jonathan Green's critical history of the twentieth century includes chapters exploring photography in popular culture and in the consciousness of its time. Roland Barthes's semiotic theories and Michel Foucault's idea that vision can impose social control have influenced most critical historians.

Many of them work from a decidedly American vantage point, discovering in photographs the evidence of predominant ideas at one place in time. For example, Alan Trachtenberg finds that, just as nineteenth-century American portraits projected a republican ideal (see Figure 2.3) that contrasted sharply with that era's view of the "other" (Figure 2.4), each succeeding period of photography contains a narrative about some American ideology. Miles Orvell uses pho-

 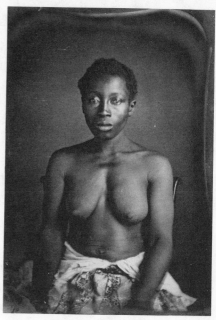

FIGURE 2.3.
Brady studio,
*Horace Greeley,
editor and
publisher,*
daguerreotype,
New York, c.
1850 (Library
of Congress).
Pl. 7 in
Trachtenberg.

FIGURE 2.4.
J. T. Zealy,
*Delia, country-
born of African
parents, daughter
of Renty,*
Congo,
daguerreotype,
Mar. 1850
(Peabody
Museum, Har-
vard). Pl. 13 in
Trachtenberg.

tography to explore how American culture separated the authentic from its imitations. James Guimond shows how photographs illustrated the idea of the American dream. Other authors explore still other ways in which ideological power operates through pictures (Bolton).

One weakness of critical theory, cited by Green and others, is that the resulting histories tend to assign privilege to language and treat images as second-rate. For example, the narratives of writers, in essays by Sontag and others, come off as much more precise and powerful than the ambiguous perceptions and creativity of photographers. Green calls the tendency to discount pictures "puritanical." Thinking of photography as completely subservient to ideology does resonate with icon smashing and may drain the power from photographs in experience. The critics would insist, however, that iconoclasm can be liberating. Journalists and critical readers who recognize how photographs, especially the strongest, most memorable ones, convey larger myths

36

may create and read pictures more thoughtfully, with more concern for their power and consequences.

*G*reat Men, Great Events, Great Pictures"

Before we turn from history to practice, we need to explore one more area. The history of photojournalism was, until recently, a minor footnote in the annals of photography, most often notable for its absence. The first histories of photojournalism were published in manuals and textbooks aimed at students and amateurs seeking to enter the profession (Kinkaid; Ezickson). The stream of handbooks that followed has produced several influential essays. The literate and philosophical work by Wilson Hicks placed photojournalism within the context of contemporary ideas. In contrast, Arthur Rothstein emphasized the technical antecedents to press photography. These and a few other books (e.g., Gidal) drew on the authors' memoirs of the field. Although sometimes more laden with historical facts, histories of photojournalism in textbooks since Hicks have rarely displayed a better grasp of the workings of change (e.g., Geraci; Kobre; Hoy).

Photojournalism history has also accumulated in the collections of pictures published in books. These include the "great" news pictures reproduced either as histories of photojournalism (e.g., Norback and Gray; Faber) or as general histories of the twentieth century (e.g., Evans, *Eyewitness;* Schuneman), the winners of competitions such as the National Press Photographers Association "bests" and the Pulitzer Prizes (e.g., *Best;* Leekley and Leekley), and portfolio collections by and about individual photojournalists (e.g., Fellig; Capa; Eisenstaedt). Newspapers, magazines, and photographic agencies have also published institutional histories with pictures (e.g., *Images;* Kee; Manchester). Some of these treat the general history of the field (e.g., Lacayo and Russell).

Finally, press pictures have on occasion played an important role in museum exhibitions, such as the Family of Man at the

Museum of Modern Art, which Edward Steichen curated in the 1950s. Several subsequent exhibits have focused specifically on the press, encouraging attention and analysis (e.g., Baynes; Fulton). The most important of these, organized by John Szarkowski, took issue with many traditions of the field (*Picture Press*). These museum exhibition catalogs contain the best early drafts of photojournalism history.

Modern photojournalism is a youngster among photographic genres, having emerged only since the 1920s. As a consequence, its first historians had to fashion a story from the selvage of other histories. For a supply of facts, they stitched together many fragments: a cursory search for the roots of visual communication in prehistoric cave paintings, the origins of photography in the camera obscura, the story of newspaper pictures from the earliest engravings and woodcuts, the history of printing halftone photographs in the press, and the growth of the photojournalism profession and wire agencies. What held these threads together was a definition of photojournalism: the depiction of real events and the promulgation of the result to a wide audience.

We march through life and behind us marches the photographer and the reporter.

— *Finley Peter Dunne*

For a supply of ideas, most of the short histories in handbooks and manuals echo the traditional picture history. From cave paintings, through the experiments of artists such as Goya and Hogarth, to modern photography, civilization supposedly overcame all the mechanical obstacles to representing factual reality. Cameras got smaller, easier to operate, and more versatile. New lenses conquered detail and distance, flashes overcame the darkness, films captured action and eventually color. With greater flexibility, photographers were able to replace the artificiality of posing with candid shots that wrote essays from events. Photojournalists were limited only by their own daring and enterprise. With photojournalism, the long progress of technology toward the classical ideal seemed to find its culmination.

The earliest accounts also revealed the facets of the story that would fascinate later writers. Technology has consistently played a dominant role. Recent textbooks have sometimes gone so far as to divide events into epochs named for equipment, such as the Speed Graphic period or the 35-mm era. Besides technical progress, the histories also build a cult of great photographers, a catalog of the historical events they covered, and a lore of the small moments captured by dint of the photojournalist's humanity or good fortune.

The many collections of historic pictures and the portfolios of noted photojournalists, agencies, and periodicals lend weight to this version of history. The canon of "great" pictures has become identified (e.g., Edom) from the winners of contests, by some connection with memorable historical events, or through shop talk, as photojournalists retell the stories of their experiences. All of these collections result from the increasing professionalization of the field. The first collections of "greats" came out of professional societies. Newspaper pictures collected as general histories do more than recount familiar events. They build the case for the importance of photojournalism and its practitioners. They also assign value to the coincidence of photographing what turns out to be historically significant, and applaud the bravery and risk taking of photojournalists.

Regardless of the philosophy driving these books, the pictures they reproduce (images of the Hindenburg exploding, or of marines taking Iwo Jima, for example) have great power, despite their overuse. The text accompanying the picture collections also displays moments of brilliance. Henri Cartier-Bresson's introduction to his collected work is the most influential example. He eloquently raises ethical and social issues with a modesty that counters the "great men" theme inherent within the context of his book and other photojournalism collections as well.

$\mathcal{T}$he History of Photojournalism

Where Cartier-Bresson's essay does not attempt history, others do. Wilson Hicks suggests that before the 1920s, photographs entered a world that had only the philosophy of painting (and of the fine graphic arts such as engraving) to supply a system for understanding pictures. Although many informational pictures were shot before then, they were little appreciated and even less understood. Editors, who resisted using photographs, had literary minds and training; for them pictures were not serious. Photographs seemed jarring in a culture not accustomed to seeing art jostling up against text. This explains why, until the early 1900s, a buffer of borders, frames, and bric-a-brac surrounded most pictures (Figure 2.5). Even as it used illustrations, the nineteenth-century picture press practiced what the newspaper designer Allen Hutt calls typography-centered journalism (Baynes).

In his introduction to the exhibition Scoop, Scandal, and Strife, Ken Baynes argues that the appearance of the first photographic tabloid in 1904 marked a change that, besides being technical, was conceptual. The editors of popular tabloids invented a new way to think about pictures. Instead of being viewed as secondary illustrations of the written text, pictures became defined as another category of content. From typographic and photographic content, editors invented a new medium, although rarely acknowledged, that

FIGURE 2.5. Front page with a turn-of-the-century press picture surrounded by a border. *New York Journal* 26 June 1905: 1.

until recently has stood in contrast to the "serious" newspaper, the preexisting typographic medium. Hutt points out that the new photographic tabloids segregated typography and photography as separate but equal forms.

These changes brought pictures into the competition for news that ruled the journalism of the time. According to Hicks, photographic competition led to coverage based on the single picture. Improved cameras, flash powders, and the picture syndicates of the early twentieth century encouraged the single shot. Smaller cameras got press photographers in and out of events faster; the clouds of smoke after the flash prevented a second shot; and rapid transmission made any delay seem like malingering. What Hicks calls the emerging "doctrine of the scoop" — getting the picture first and beating the competition into print — also encouraged imitation. Photographers in a hurry produced a steady stream of group lineups, mug shots, and the like. Although smaller, cameras in the early 1900s were still large, and pictures were valued principally for sharpness and reproducibility. A photographer entering the room dominated the scene, so that people stopped, looked at the camera, and either arranged themselves or raised objections. In contrast to the stiffness of those posing, the press photographer acquired the stereotype, in popular depictions, of resembling an "unkempt and evil-smelling animal" (Hicks 10).

Modern photojournalism emerged in the 1920s and 1930s because of changes in the attitudes and ideas surrounding the press. According to Raymond Williams, greater circulation promotion, new modes of advertising, and the concentration of industrial ownership led to visual changes in newspapers. The new mass culture, emerging after the Great War of 1914–18, held convenience and efficiency as central aims. Hicks suggests that these ideas contributed to the popularity of the camera and altered the way photojournalists worked. The small and speedy Leica, marketed in this setting, could reduce camera procedures to reflexes, make sequences of pic-

Figure 2.6.
Advertisement
for the Leica.
T. J. Maloney,
*U.S. Camera,
1940* (New
York:
Random
House, 1938).

—the Universal Camera for every photographic purpose!

tures practical, and increase the likelihood of getting a good shot (Figure 2.6). The relationship between photographer and people also changed. As cameras became less obtrusive, photographers could take pictures without the cooperation of their subjects. A cultural commitment to ease and efficiency worked to the photojournalist's advantage. By not startling the statesmen of the League of Nations, photographer Erich Salomon managed to startle readers accustomed to stilted, one-shot coverage of diplomacy.

Salomon and the founders of modern photojournalism changed not only their mode of operation but also the resulting form of pictures. Compared with the results of one-shot coverage, candid photographs required less sharpness and reproducibility. Pictures became valued as carriers of both detail *and* emotion. Szarkowski characterizes modern photojournalism as seemingly frank, favoring emotion over intellect and emphasizing the subjective, while redefining privacy and narrowing anonymity (see Figure 2.7). These modern pictures also took great authority from their emotional power and ostensibly

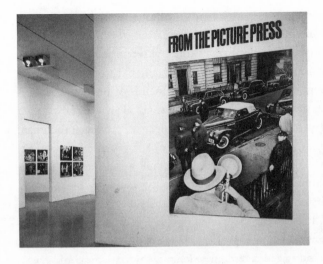

FIGURE 2.7. Exhibition photograph. John Szarkowski, *From the Picture Press* (New York: MoMA, 1973).

objective detail. The picture seemed to be the news in itself. According to Hicks, *Time* and *Life* magazines adopted new attitudes toward photographs. Editors subjected every picture to serious critical attention and refused to retouch the print or decorate its borders. Photographs became integrated with text and treated as its equal. Like words, pictures could supply a core of information and could join together to form stories. These beliefs led editors to make photographs larger and to present them in series as essays.

The changes in the treatment of pictures eventually improved the status of photojournalists, who could command respect not only in the industry but also in museums. The exhibitions beginning in the 1950s did not merely accept the "great men, great pictures" bias of the profession. In *From the Picture Press*, Szarkowski rejects historic pictures as mere strokes of luck. The preponderance of what photojournalists spend their professional lives producing is of another sort, he writes. Seen as a whole, press pictures contain a kaleidoscopic flow of particular faces within a few permanent roles. Szarkowski, with the aid of Diane Arbus, among others, selected the most "compelling" and "original" pictures, judged by their formal and iconographic contribution to this vocabulary of roles. The organization of the exhibit demonstrated a few of these roles: participants in ceremony, the loser and the winner, victims of disaster, the bizarre, partakers in the good life, the contestant, the hero. These roles display something akin to what Barthes calls "canonic generality" (Thompson). Szarkowski shows that the specific, local particularity of the news picture is ideal for displaying these general structures.

Besides filling permanent roles with transient faces, photojournalism also fills pages, manufacturing from daily events sufficient pictures to fulfill the demands of printing machinery, reader interests, and advertising. How the newspaper industry organizes its work can affect its product (Tuchman; Fishman). In the case of photojournalism, Szarkowski observes that the function of coverage has dictated the form of pictures. Early in the century, for example, by selecting certain equipment, photojournalists depicted a world in which most events happened twelve feet from the camera. In any newspaper, the greatest share of pictures show planned events and staged ceremonies. Even so, as Szarkowski observes, the meanings of individual shots are not so clear as we may assume or as the captions may suggest.

The study and reading of photojournalism history seems all the more urgent because recent books and exhibitions have largely returned to the "great men, great pictures" tradition (e.g., Fulton; Lacayo and Russell). The early practical handbooks included history to illustrate the exertions of publishers and inventors to make pictures reproducible in newspapers. The lessons of history were these: Pictures made newspapers more competitive; pictures increased circulation. Without photojournalism, publishers could not achieve journalistic greatness. In the 1970s, with the picture magazines folding, textbook histories renewed these claims and offered photojournalism as the response to television. History has been put to many uses, polemical as well as instrumental. As in so much else, Hicks gave the most persuasive reason to understand pictures in history: One must examine how photos were used and regarded before in order to understand the attitudes and uses of photojournalism today.

Playing Photographer

*T*his exercise, extremely simple as photography, requires a high level of awareness and keen self-observation to be effective. As you work through the exercise, watch carefully and remember each thing you and those around you do. The exercise is simply this: Take your camera to a public place, such as a shopping district or a park, and shoot pictures of a half-dozen people you don't know.

Almost any camera will do. An instant camera avoids the delay of developing film, but you may find yourself consciously altering the way you shoot as you inspect each picture. If you use an instant camera, set the pictures aside for examining later. Use a camera you are familiar with or one that requires the least possible technical skill. If you don't own and can't borrow a camera, pick up a disposable one. Slide film works well and can be developed quickly and inexpensively. When you have filled a roll, get the film developed at a quick-processing shop.

In the course of shooting the pictures, take three views of each person. Make each view as different from the others as possible. You can get different views not only by following the person to different locations, but also by changing the way you frame the person (close up or far away) and by varying the angle you shoot from (high or low).

While you wait for your film, find a place free of distractions, and carefully reconstruct the experience in writing. Describe each thing you did from the moment you arrived at the chosen public place. Detail exactly what people around you did. Report any overheard conversations or reactions, and write out any dialogue that passed between you and the strangers you met. Include whatever information you learned about any of them. Take pains to make as complete a record as possible.

Also write down your intellectual and emotional responses at each phase of the experience. What did you think about? Reconstruct your thought processes and the ideas that occurred to you as you worked. How did you explain your actions to yourself? Recall in minute detail your feelings when you began, when you took pictures, when any conversations occurred, and when the roll was full. Be honest and thorough, carefully avoiding the urge either to embroider and exaggerate or to understate and censor your reactions.

Then turn to your developed slides or prints. Do not begin by criticizing them. Instead, pick one or two pictures, and write captions for them. You may make your selection following any criteria — those you know the most about, prefer for some reason, or choose at random. Write the captions any way you like: with a fact list, an anecdote, a quotation, a descriptive sentence, or any combination. The length is also up to you. As you make these decisions, jot down your reasons for each one.

Codes of Composition

The techniques photographers employ, the pictures they produce, and the social settings where they work fall into several genres. Fine-art photographers produce pictures for display in museums and galleries and for sale to collectors. Technical photographers fill the instrumental demand for aerial, architectural, and medical pictures and the like. Commercial work divides between photographers who work for businesses, doing advertising and promotion, and those who work in retail studios, doing weddings and portraits. Documentary photographers most often work for the media.

Within the documentary genre, photojournalism follows a formal code of composition that can be found in the photographs themselves but is expressed explicitly in textbooks and manuals (Schwartz). The earliest handbooks (e.g., Price; Pouncey) generally advise against conscious composition. They equate composing with the work of academicians, arguing that "one cannot do much arranging of lighting and subject matter with spot news" (Vitray, Mills, and Ellard 132). Another early writer, James Kinkaid, says formal composition doesn't interest news photographers and applauds their resistance to artistic pictures and salon exhibitions.

Yet these early handbooks still contain a formal compositional code. Kinkaid lists several rules: Center the action in the frame, shoot big scenes high enough to leave the foreground uncluttered, correct the leaning effect of tall buildings, get principal things large in the frame, and keep the composition simple. All of these, except the now-abandoned rule on centering, have long been axiomatic in news photography. Although they advise against composition, the early handbooks insist that experience is the only way to learn photojournalism, that an innate sense of composition comes only from the alchemy of living. Short of that, students can read books on visual composition and spend time observing photos and paintings.

Photojournalism began with ambivalence toward aesthetic concerns. While not wanting to approach the affectations of fine-art photography, photojournalists still needed to differentiate their practices from what amateurs did. The middle ground they found — unacknowledged composing hidden behind the mystery of professional experience — has been noted in the sociological literature (Rosenblum). Although some critics insist that the anti-aesthetic still rules (Brecheen-Kirkton), later practitioner handbooks began to favor composition. By the 1960s, ideas from modern art and from advertising had filtered into photojournalism. From modern art came an emphasis on formal order and on visual expression. Several authors list the elements of art and design (e.g., Spencer). They consider form an expression of dignity, serenity, comfort, pleasure, and the like. From advertising came the well-known set of design principles (see Chapter 5 on layout). Some textbooks cite studies to show that conscious visual composition enhances the appeal of pictures to readers, increasing the circulation and the prestige of the newspaper (e.g., Fox and Kerns).

From these ideas, photojournalism by the 1980s appears to have established a code of composition based on simplicity, economy, and asymmetry (Bergin; Kerns). To achieve simplicity, textbooks recommend that photojournalists choose a single center of interest, framed so that the background does not interfere. Unlike human eyesight, a camera can record backgrounds with as much detail as foregrounds, and the camera's lack of bifocal depth collapses distances into a single plane. To edit the background, photojournalists move around the subject, so that within the frame, no lamps or poles sprout from the body (see Figure 2.8). Or they may control the depth of field to blur the background. To achieve economy, the textbooks advise filling up the frame. This can be done by moving close in while shooting. Or photographers can use zoom lenses to get the effect of close-in shots. Economical pictures also avoid dead space between subjects and exclude details extraneous to the center of interest. To achieve asymmetry, the texts advise photojournalists to compose shots away from center. Every recent book explains the "rule of thirds," which divides the

FIGURE 2.8. Art challenging a textbook convention of composition. John Baldessari, *Wrong*, 1967. John Baldessari Exhibition, Whitney Museum of American Art, 1991.

frame into three parts, both vertically and horizontally. The resulting grid is like a tic-tac-toe game, with the center block usually off limits.

These modernist compositional strategies have spread in part through the influence of the photography industry, which has distributed manuals and books teaching the modern recipe for good pictures (Schwartz and Griffin). Despite the generally recognized separation of photojournalism from other genres, a photographer switching from one genre to another would find substantial similarity among the genres' vocabularies of form. Like the general recommendations of camera makers, the advice in photojournalism textbooks primarily seeks to differentiate the professional from the amateur photograph.

Your own pictures probably follow the code of amateur snapshots. You may have put the important figure in the middle. Snapshots are often centered. Your subjects may appear stiff or static, looking into the camera. Snapshots often look posed. If you did catch people in action, they may be looking away from the camera. Unposed snapshots often catch random-looking moments. You may also have shown little concern for the surrounding background, leaving large margins of space and many unrelated details. Snapshots set up social distances, especially between strangers, and often envelop people in a buffer or in clutter. On the whole, snapshots tend to give an impression of awkwardness or timidity, in contrast to the aggressiveness of the close-in press photo.

 diting Pictures

When newspapers use amateur pictures of events, the image must be edited. Picture editing has become the specialty of newspaper staff supervisors, with a related field of study in college courses and textbooks (e.g., Evans, *Pictures;* McDougall and Hampton; Hurley and McDougall). The editing of any picture, whether a snapshot or not, involves four main procedures. The picture must be selected, sized and shaped ("cropped") to fit into the newspaper, and laid out on a page, and its caption must be written. All of these procedures get close attention in picture-editing textbooks. Editing your captions and cropping your own pictures will give you some insight into the process.

First, consider your caption. The words people write on the backs of snapshots or on the pages of photo albums may identify who is in the picture, when it was taken, and perhaps where. Commercial photographs only rarely identify the photographer or the details in the frame. Advertisers play the product and brand name prominently, usually without naming the models. If written to accompany a work of art photography, a legend usually emphasizes the name of the artist, along with any title, date, and so forth. After giving credit to individual creativity, fine-art legends often leave the rest — the who, what, when, and where within the photograph — open to interpretation.

The study of the relationships between words and images has generally focused on the arts and literature (e.g., Hunter), but photojournalism has long been closely tied to language (Whiting; Rhode and McCall). Journalistic captions use a set of language conventions entirely different from those followed in art. Instead of dealing with the picture as individual, authored work, press captions go directly to the manifest content in the image. The picture is brought into the world of news with a sentence naming the individuals depicted, telling what they are doing, specifying when they (not the photographer) did what they did, and where. The photographer's name, if it appears at all, is set smaller than regular reading text and arranged unobtrusively, often turned on its side. The type and layout reinforce the importance of the content, not the author.

Besides identifying the "who, what, when, and where," journalistic captions often amplify the picture's meaning with another descriptive sentence or two. Barthes says that the text has now begun to illustrate the news image, rather than the other way around, when older types of images illustrated the text. Some research has verified the dominance of the picture (Fedler, Counts, and Hightower). One assumption behind captions is that a picture reflects reality, which can be named and described. A caption that depends on the image also shares in its objectivity. As Stuart Hall has suggested, however, the caption conveys one particular interpretation, which ties the picture not only into news values but also into the larger myths of the culture. In other words, captions restate what a photograph shows and also imply what it is about: the issues, problems, and beliefs it raises.

Behold the whole huge earth sent to me hebdomadally in a brown-paper wrapper!

— *James Russell Lowell*

⌘ Your own captions might be rewritten to conform to the conventions of photojournalism. In one sentence, you would name whoever appears in the picture (unless there are more than five in a group) and tell what they're doing and when and where they did it. A second sentence might provide a quotation or additional information about the people or events to make them seem present and real. To write that sort of caption, you would need to have taken the picture with the caption in mind. How would your experience have been different? The act of shooting might have been altered, and you certainly would have needed to converse with any individual whose picture you took. Would their responses have been different as well? The journalistic enterprise changes every aspect of the picture, actively creating one version of reality.

Next, consider your photographs. Books on editing generally adhere to the guidelines of picture composition taught to photojournalists. With that knowledge, editors can scale the image to fit into the newspaper. They can also crop the picture's edges to fit into the available space and to focus attention on some portion of the image, while improving the composition. Scaling and cropping often change a picture dramatically, and editing books give numerous examples of bad and better results. Many of the rules are mechanical. For example, the books recommend against cropping off body parts at the joints, especially the knees and elbows, but also at the waist and neck. They also suggest using cropping to square up the edges of buildings and make tall things vertical and the horizon horizontal. To allow for what is called the vector (the implied or anticipated direction of a gaze or action frozen by the camera), the books recommend that space be left in front of anything photographed in motion. Editors may also crop off the subject's back or trailing limbs in an action shot.

Textbooks sometimes contrast these conventions with snapshots. Amateurs often show the entire figure and usually do not control for visual vectors. Things in a snapshot are often slightly askew. Although news pictures are defined by content and other considerations, your snapshots can be turned into something close to press pictures by cropping. Use slips of paper to recompose the picture, covering up the edges so that the subject fills the frame and is positioned away from the center. The result may not have the candid quality and edited background of a professional shot, but even following a few of the rules may succeed in encoding the picture as photojournalism. If you had been aware of formal composition codes, would you have shot your pictures any differently? Compare the versions of your pictures and captions before and after editing. Did the editing make the image better? Did the new composition and caption lend the picture an air of authority, value, or interest? The procedures followed by picture editors add another level of complexity to the understanding of photojournalism.

*P*icture Narratives

Photojournalism also tells stories, and the narrative dimension explains part of its power. The photojournalist *takes* pictures by removing people's images from the sites of lived experience. A photojournalist also *makes* pictures by moving about, composing the shots, and superimposing a preconceived story plan. By coming up with story ideas and then taking and making pictures, photojournalists weave people's images into the tapestry of news. Editors also join in by giving assignments and then choosing pictures, in a process that both defines and manufactures the news (Gans; Gitlin). Like other narratives, news includes characters and a story line or plot.

First, consider how photojournalists take pictures from the scene of an event. Taking a picture removes people from the flow of their lives and makes them into characters. The act does more than record; it influences the characterization.

> *I* write
> from the
> worm's eye
> point of view.
>
> — *Ernie Pyle*

Photographic reporters conceal themselves only with difficulty, and their presence can affect the scene. People behave differently before witnesses, and especially before a camera, whether the differences result from shyness or dramatics. A photojournalist can't remain entirely unobtrusive and neutral. Even without thinking, people respond by arranging themselves before the camera.

Photojournalists use a variety of techniques to prevent or disguise this response to the camera. A candid shot can avoid the stiff or antic reactions of the subject, as can a picture made with a telephoto lens. An action shot, with the subject too absorbed to pay attention, likewise prevents much reaction to the camera. These techniques work by eliminating the subject's participation, at least until after the shot has been taken. Photojournalists opposed to staged shooting may eschew any picture with subjects looking at the camera. Other photojournalists try to achieve the same natural effect by intervening actively in the scene. They may spend time talking, coaching, or suggesting a pose or an action to put the subject at ease. With real patience, they can all but eliminate the self-conscious reactions of subjects.

These two approaches have sparked a controversy among photojournalists over whether pictures should be set up, and the debate has defined an ethical domain within the profession (Lester). Some authors object to the practice, arguing that any posing should be made obvious or mentioned explicitly in the caption to avoid misleading the reader. Some photojournalists have lost their jobs for going too far to pose subjects. However, other authors consider a little stage direction essential in many cases. Even in the absence of verbal instructions, photojournalists may communicate their intentions and needs through eye contact, nods, smiles, and other body language (Henderson). Practitioners may use both approaches, shooting unannounced when they think it appropriate and intervening when they need the subject's cooperation.

Intervention in the scene seems to be more of an issue for breaking or "spot" news, events commonly supposed to be spontaneous. General news photographs, in contrast, come from planned events that newsmakers routinely set up. The widely held distinction between spot and general news has become embedded in the categories and prizes of news picture contests. However, all types of events can be covered in an established, conventional order, following something akin to the plot of an opera or a sitcom. To understand the procedure, consider next how the photojournalist makes pictures.

Whether the event is general or spot news, editors expect photojournalists to anticipate what to shoot and then to plan ahead of time. Textbooks call this planning "pre-visualizing" (Kerns). The procedure helps make shooting routine, so that the photojournalist can efficiently extract images from their settings to create a news narrative. The textbooks identify several stock narratives: the speech or meeting, the breaking

FIGURE 2.9. Narrative conventions of news picture stories. Bob Lynn, *Virginian-Pilot* and *Ledger-Star* 1 Apr. 1980. Fig. 18.14 in Hoy 201.

news of an arrest or a fire, the weather, and so forth. Although the details change, the stories can follow the same overall structure. Textbooks list the typical shots that make up a picture story (Figure 2.9). One made from above or at a distance sets the scene, several intermediate shots capture the action, a close-up conveys emotion, and so forth. This logical procedure helps the photojournalist succeed under the pressure of deadlines and the flow of events.

By following the standard approach, photojournalists may unintentionally reiterate a set of beliefs about people. As played out in photo essays, the planned shots often assume a hero and a victim. The scene is set, the hero takes action, and the victim expresses emotion. The narrative teaches that the world is not safe, that when things go wrong what is needed is a hero to intervene and set them right. And the need for a hero presumes a victim, someone who waits passively for rescue. A politician visiting the scene of disaster assumes the hero's role, announcing solutions or denouncing opponents or other evils. The victims can then demonstrate their emotional responses. This narrative permeates and defines many news stories but may or may not square with the subjects' experiences of the events.

Conventional narratives allow society to manage the cacophony of daily life, defining some events as newsworthy and others as trivial. Editors and press photographers partici-pate, and, although they don't entirely control the process, they need to understand how their participation creates, as well as reports, the news. Photojournalists may not consider their own work quite so purposeful, but the planning and direction come clear in comparison with amateur snapshots.

When you shot three pictures of the same stranger, you gathered raw materials that can now be turned into a narra-tive. Examine your pictures to see if the strangers responded to the camera by acting (posturing, posing artificially, "ham-ming it up") or by becoming stiff and reserved. In your three pictures, did you intervene, or shoot without talking? Why did you choose your approach? Although you may not have realized it, you took sides in the debate about setting up pic-tures. Did your decision affect the way your pictures turned out? The subject might have adopted a different posture before the camera if you had acted differently. Try lining the pictures up and inventing a story to explain the three shots in order. Then rearrange the pictures and make up another story to match. Although you had the freedom to fabricate, how much were your stories influenced by what you actually saw? Did your imagination affect your judgment or opinion of the stranger? Working with your pictures of strangers can give you insight into the way narratives get fashioned, although they seem to spring from events.

The Ethics of Photojournalism

Your own reactions contain the most telling insights into the experience of shooting strangers. Review your notes to recall how you felt and responded. Did the exercise require you to do things that seemed rude or awkward? How did you manage those feelings? Your method of initi-ating the picture taking is especially important. Did you introduce yourself first or shoot first? Did you smile, nod, and appear friendly? Or did you try to look professional and serious? If you talked to your subjects, how much did you learn about them? Did that information change your initial attitude toward them? How did you manage negative or hostile subjects? Also consider the pictures and your reactions to them. Do they seem accurate depictions of what happened between you and the strangers? Did you feel empowered by the experience? By taking pictures in public, you confronted personally several issues: the power of the photojournalist, the power of the subject, and the power of the image.

Scholarly research into photojournalism falls into categories much like these three. A majority of studies analyze the press picture for its technique, form, or content (e.g., Lester and Smith). Some researchers observe the photojournalist or picture editor through surveys, descriptions, and the like (e.g., Bethune). A few experiments consider the audience, focusing on how readers respond to content or form (e.g., Wanta). Notably absent from this list is any direct study of the condition of the people in the pictures. Simple convenience may explain why. Pictures are readily accessible artifacts for study; readers are right at hand; even distant practitioners can be found and surveyed. But the citizens actually shown in pictures exist at a great remove from the printed page. They neither share a common geography nor belong to a single mailing list.

Although their methods tend to ignore the people in pictures, most researchers do address pictorial content. They most often measure the picture, the photojournalist, or the audience in light of some contemporary controversy over gender, race, politics, war, shocking images, or the like. The pictured citizen, although unnamed and without voice in the studies, is represented as a member of a group (the categories of women and African Americans appear most frequently in this research). As scholars try to document how a group is treated visually, they generally conclude that one of a triumvirate of ethical standards will ultimately safeguard the citi-zen-as-group-member.

From the perspective of photojournalism ethics (Lester), one safeguard of citizens' rights is the photojournalist's commitment to truth. In the discussions of ethics, truth depends first on the definition of the photograph as a reliable document and second on the integrity of that photographic image. To avoid falsehood, photojournalists can prohibit such activities as manipulating the film by assembling, removing, or adjusting the people and things depicted. Retouching appeared almost as early as photography itself but required time and skill and could usually be detected. Digital images remove those obstacles, so that almost anyone with a personal computer can remove or add people, change their appearance, and recast events, sometimes without leaving a trace. The advent of digital photography has been met by an outpouring of debate and scholarship on ethics (*Photojournalism Ethics*).

Another safeguard of citizens' rights is the legal guarantee of privacy. Under U.S. law, pictures taken in public places must not invade the people's privacy by appropriation, intrusion, publication of private matters, or false light, or by the separate but related law of libel. Appropriation occurs when a citizen's images are used for trade or advertising without permission. Photographers taking pictures for commercial uses must obtain a release signed by the person depicted. Intrusion occurs when the photographer shoots pictures, without permission, of people in private places. Your home or secluded backyard would be off limits, for example. Publication of private matters occurs when photographers expose facts the public has no need to know. Although public figures are subjected to closer personal scrutiny, mere curiosity is not a compelling need. False light occurs when a photograph is used, with or without a release, to imply something untrue about the citizen. Libel occurs when pictures expose a person to ridicule, contempt, or hatred. The traditional defense for libel is truth. These legal limits on publishing press photographs are found in the literature of libel and privacy in communications law.

Because respecting privacy rights and photographic integrity does not necessarily make a picture acceptable for publication, editors have developed a third safeguard to protect the citizen-subject: community standards of taste and decency. Photographers sometimes get pictures that editors consider offensive, depicting violence, grief, death, nudity, or sexual activity. These images generally are proscribed because they draw an angry reaction from readers, who write or call to complain particularly about nearby events pictured in a morning edition (Baker). Editors may buck that reaction if they believe the news, however offensive, serves the public good. For example, violent pictures sometimes get justified because their shock value may encourage public caution or prevention. These decisions usually produce a lively argument in the professional press and feed another area of ethical debate among photojournalists (MacDougall).

The bounds of taste and decency common to the audience, along with the honesty of the photojournalist and the privacy and libel laws that surround publication of the photograph, build an ethics of photojournalism on the same three footings beneath the traditional histories and empirical studies on photojournalism. Together, the ethical groundwork presumably protects the rights of citizens who become subjects in press pictures.

Critical Practice

Critical scholars since the 1970s have challenged these foundation stones of photojournalism ethics. At the heart of the critique lies the definition of truth. Sociologists and anthropologists, among others, have questioned whether photographs have any special claim to truth (Becker; Worth).

Critical historians have cast doubt on the documentary reliability of photojournalism (Hardt; Brecheen-Kirkton). Accepting the need for skepticism, several scholars have hinted at ways that photojournalism can be practiced in light of this postmodern critique (Jensen; Sekula, "War"; Phelan). Although these studies call into question common assumptions about truth, privacy, and taste, they do not seem to cast doubt on the importance of pictures in the newspaper.

A society has no hope of governing what it cannot see. And in our relatively short history, the institution of the free press has become not only America's eye but its mirror.

— James Squires

🖾 Critical scholars agree with the photojournalists and ethicists who say that electronic cameras and digital storage may largely erase the reliability of photographs as evidence. But the critics go further. They point to a host of darkroom procedures that photojournalists routinely use to manipulate images with the old technologies. Lenses, films, and photographic processes themselves alter the image, and photojournalism has consistently used or adjusted for these changes. Critics also list the many ways photojournalists arrange the content of pictures by choosing what to shoot and moving around to position it in the frame. When ethicists sound the alarm about digital photography, the critics argue, what gets lost is the fundamental question about truth: Whose reality — whose version of truth — gets shown?

🖾 Privacy laws have also come under criticism. The legal breaches of privacy on the standard list — appropriation, intrusion, and so forth — all spring from the definition of the images as a commodity. The rules governing control of images divide the commodity into two classes according to use. Images used in advertising and promotion are the property of the individuals depicted, to sell or trade away. Those used in editorial matter are free for the taking, with the caveat that the publisher must respect the truth. But focusing on the right to use pictures obscures the ethical conundrum of whether one has the right to take a picture (Henderson). The issue can be illustrated by the difference between words and images. When approached by reporters, sources may choose to speak or remain silent. Once the source speaks, the writer may quote freely. Not so with images. Sources' nonverbal speech, encoded in dress, gesture, and posture and in their surroundings and physical attributes, gets used without regard to their wishes (Figure 2.10). The right to remain silent does not exist in the court of images.

Critical scholars have also objected to the ethical appeal to community tastes. Newspapers commonly circulate among many groups whose standards diverge widely. Some cultures accept nudity and expressions of grief in some settings more than others do. Critics point out that what is tolerable in an image showing outsiders may become intolerable if the image shows insiders. The display of mutilated or dead bodies, for example, may be more acceptable if the bodies come from other races or distant places. This defining of "us" and "them," especially in pictures, can depend on subjects' physical appearance, overemphasizing attributes such as race, deformity, or fashion. American photojournalists are usually white, male, and

FIGURE 2.10. Clothing code of group identity. Hal Fischer, "Street Fashion, Basic Gay," *Gay Semiotics: A Photographic Study of Visual Coding among Homosexual Men* (San Francisco: NFS P, 1977) 46, fig. 19.

college educated (Bethune). As a practical matter, they are more comfortable shooting in groups where they can blend in. A photojournalist whose presence cannot be passed off as normal and ordinary influences how people act and are in turn shown (Henderson). The community may then object to its depiction on grounds of taste that differ greatly from what editors may assume.

Several authors suggest that photojournalists can still prosper in a culturally diverse world. Editors can choose pictures that break stereotypes and patterns (Phelan). Photojournalists can seek assignments to cover groups and individuals who remain invisible or "silent" in most coverage (Brecheen-Kirkton). Institutional reform may be needed before we see many changes in the patterns of creating news, but photojournalists can influence the changes. Before shooting, a photojournalist can acknowledge individuals' need to control their images by taking the time to learn and understand their beliefs and values and by trying to make pictures that reflect their view of themselves. The empathy and social awareness required to make these pictures can also be a part of the photojournalist's training (Kerns). Finally, critics have a place in exploring where photojournalism founders, becoming a captive of institutions and its own practices. The best recent example of this is the critique of coverage during the Persian Gulf conflict (Sekula, "War"; Hardt; Phelan).

Journalism allows its readers to witness history.

— John Hersey

What the advocates of photojournalism ethics and their critics share with photojournalists themselves is the belief that the pictures in newspapers are extremely powerful. The still image has entered the cultural memory as an artifact of history. Its objectivity, however much debated, is secondary to its symbolism. Pictures of the Germans tearing apart the Berlin Wall or the lone Chinese protester blocking a line of tanks in Beijing form a common heritage, a shared memory that transcends national boundaries. Historic pictures may not be the daily stock-in-trade of the photojournalist, but they are symbols of the profession, an overriding reason why people enter the field (Burnett). Although rare, these pictures have a lasting effect on society. The ideological power of the still image, which so alarms critics, also makes pictures worth criticizing.

The conventions of photojournalism have evolved through its history. But the mature profession cannot remain the same. Its ethics since the 1920s have depended on respect for the photographic print, a form that may soon become the province of fine artists. Its codes of content and conventions of form are being co-opted by advertising. The controversial Benetton advertisements, which use journalistic shots of war, people with AIDS, and environmental issues with no explanation beyond the company logo, are but one of many examples (Berger). Not only will the next generation change how photojournalists compose and process pictures; readers and practitioners will together redefine the photojournalistic imagination, the ideas and values behind the pictures they make. Newspapers must encourage these changes if they are to hold the interest and loyalty of readers.

CHAPTER 3

My oldest son began reading the newspaper at age twelve. He

CRITIQUING

said he wanted to be an astrophysicist and then spent time

poring over the charts in the science section. His reading was

CHARTS

intermittent. When the charts caught his eye, he would read

them (but not the accompanying story), or he would tear out

the page and put it in his room. He also read the comics

more or less regularly, but he didn't pay daily attention to

FIGURE 3.1.
Chart as news.
Detroit News
17 Jan. 1991: 1.

front pages until the newspapers began publishing charts about the 1991 Gulf conflict in the Middle East (Figure 3.1). The maps with their sweeping arrows showing the advance of American troops and the diagrams comparing the military hardware of the United States and Iraq—these charts he examined in great detail each day they appeared. Then he would converse about the war, his talk peppered with military euphemisms and technical jargon, with anyone who would listen.

These one-sided conversations resembled the occasions when he would hold forth on video games, with their battles and strategies. The lives of the video-game heroes were cheap—four or five for a quarter—and games involved an intricate cost-benefit analysis that measured how many obstacles got defeated or opponents zapped for how many quarters. Like other forms of graphic information, video games seem to be based in the neutral and accurate realm of numbers and measurement. The semiotician Jacques Bertin described charts as monosemic, that is, signs customarily given only one interpretation or meaning. If two plus two always equals four, then numbers are not open to subjective interpretations. His semiotics seems to embrace the fallacy that because numbers are monosemic, their two-dimensional or visual display must also be so.

But, like the video games my son played, the tables,

graphs, maps, and diagrams of the Gulf conflict (in fact, charts of any sort) are signs every bit as rich in significance as language. The etymology of charts springs from their history and contemporary uses. These meanings are multifarious; they do diverse cultural work. Charts are signs of commerce and wealth, of military might, of technological change, and of the political order. Behind the seeming objectivity of counting, measurement, and statistics lies a host of conventional assumptions about how the world works and about what matters. Current practice in journalism ignores these underlying issues, editing instead for superficial conformity to the emerging industry standards.

Newspaper charts and the graphics of the video game are both arrayed in two dimensions, and both embellish most information with stereotypical decorations (Figure 3.2). The illustrations accompanying newspaper charts have been the focus of an ongoing debate among journalists and scholars (Tufte, *Envisioning Information* and *Visual Display*). Although industry standards may help prevent the gross errors that illustration sometimes introduces, they miss the point. Designing, editing, or reading charts should be an exercise not only in checking stylistic conformity but also in teasing out the

FIGURE 3.2. Chart as video game. Booklet cover, After Burner game, Genesis Master System, Sega, Inc.

underlying values. Whether charts of the Gulf conflict accurately display strategy and firepower is less significant than what they say about nature and the land, what they teach about technology, and what they imply about people, those under attack on the ground as well as those in the air.

The graphic information published during the Gulf conflict was an expression of the mood of the times. The ease with which my son's talk moved between video games and war games has had many parallels in media commentary about events in the Gulf and earlier conflicts (Hallin, "'Uncensored War'" and "Cartography"). War graphics were part of a recent resurgence in the popularity of charts, the latest of several recurring periods of statistical enthusiasm that began in the nineteenth century. Charts may again prove to be a passing fancy; even so, newspapers can establish graphic standards that deal with core values. Besides meeting technical standards for accuracy, well-designed and -edited charts could also allow for diversity, seek balance and fairness, and acknowledge the agendas they serve.

Although charts are usually produced by a single department at newspapers, all sorts of graphic information come under the rubric, including maps, diagrams, tabular matter, and statistical graphs. These forms were invented in widely divergent cultures at moments in history separated by millennia. Different professions claim each of these forms as their special province, and separate fields of study are the keepers of each historical tradition. An overview of these histories can provide some background useful in interpreting the significance of charts in newspapers.

Ancient Maps and Diagrams

Cartographers have compiled the most extensive histories (e.g., Tooley; Wilford; Crone) in any of these fields, as well as specific studies (e.g., Robinson). Mapmaking can also boast several visual histories, such as a slide library, *History of Cartography*, and a television series, The Shape of the World (Berthon and Robinson). These accounts suggest that maps have existed from the earliest of times in a variety of cultures. Scratches in the dirt that represented locations on some larger terrain were probably the first maps. Many early peoples inscribed maps on hides or stone showing nearby places. Distance was measured in travel time, and direction in relation to the rising and setting sun. Maps in ancient Egypt preserved boundaries that were washed away by the periodic flooding of the Nile. Early Assyrian maps from c. 3800 B.C.E. and Babylonian maps of the fifth century B.C.E. survived on clay tablets, as did maps from China etched on stone in the twelfth century C.E.

Cartographic tradition credits the first Greek map to Anaximander, who lived from 610 to c. 540 B.C.E. The Greeks adapted mapmaking from the Babylonians and put maps into the service of seafaring trade. Information from merchants and sailors contributed the basic data used by Ptolemy, whose scientific geography was preserved by Byzantine and Arab geographers. For the Romans, maps served as a tool of conquest, principally describing roads and colonies. Medieval sea charts of the thirteenth century recorded directions from the mariner's compass, which had come into use a century earlier (from a technology, the lodestone, that had been known for centuries). But it was the practical Roman road map that most influenced medieval cartography until the geography of Ptolemy was translated into Latin in the fifteenth century.

The 1459 world map of Fra Mauro marked the transition from medieval to early modern cartography and the shift from Italian to Portuguese dominance (Figure 3.3). The Italian city-states that controlled the spice trade had become an important center for cartography. As the Portuguese explored the coast of Africa, they began to make maps that recorded latitudes observed with the quadrant and the astro-

FIGURE 3.3.
Mapping the
center of
power. Fra
Mauro, *World
Map* (detail),
1459
(Biblioteca
Nazionale
Marciana,
Venice). No.
41 of *History of
Cartography*.

labe, adapted for use at sea. Upon reaching the Indian Ocean, they found a thriving shipping fleet that used maps to supply the spice trade. The indigenous knowledge of winds and coastlines was absorbed into European cartography and credited to the heirs of Henry the Navigator.

When the Dutch overtook the Portuguese in trade with the East, Amsterdam became the principal mapmaking city. Later, in France, under the strong centralized government of Louis XIV, home minister Jean-Baptiste Colbert arranged the founding of the Académie Royale des Sciences with a principal aim of improving maps. The French then fixed the prime meridian at Paris. When England became a powerful trade and cartographic center, the meridian was permanently established in Greenwich. Subsequent refinements in mapmaking benefitted from more accurate timepieces and surveying instruments and from the advent, in the twentieth century, of aerial and satellite photography, aided by radio and radar, and of digital computer-generated maps.

A graphic form almost as old as maps is the diagram. The development of diagrams has been studied primarily by engineers. Most standard general histories of engineering (e.g.,

Armytage; Gregory; Kirby et al.) discuss diagrams only in passing, but a few do provide more detail (Landels; Hill). The subspecialty of engineering graphics has also produced textbooks (e.g., Steidel and Henderson; Rising, Almfeldt, and DeJong; Giesecke et al.) with a general historical overview of diagrams. The best summary of the history of engineering graphics is by the historian Eugene S. Ferguson.

Most accounts suggest that the earliest diagrams to survive are from Mesopotamia. Gudea, a minor Chaldean ruler from about 2200 B.C.E., is claimed by engineers as the first of their profession. Statues show him holding materials for drafting and seated with a diagram on his lap. Another early diagram is a ground plan chiseled in stone of the Ziggurat of Ur, a tiered Sumerian temple whose ruins still stand in Iraq. An often-reproduced Egyptian tomb drawing from c. 1800 B.C.E. explains the elaborate process of moving a huge statue. Nine pairs of workers pulled each of four ropes attached to the statue, while a water-pourer lubricated the skids. Three other workers carried materials and three carried water, all of them under the supervision of a foreman. A similar pattern can be found in an Assyrian drawing (see Figure 3.9, p. 82).

These examples demonstrate the two types of diagrams developed by early civilizations: the *elevation*, or observer's view, and the *plan*, or bird's-eye view. Although none of the plans from the Greeks or Romans have survived, bronze instruments — rules, compasses, and dividers — used for drafting were unearthed at Pompeii. The Roman architect Vetruvius describes the use of instruments for making diagrams in his architectural treatise of 30 B.C.E. These techniques were probably used by the builders who invented the mechanical devices of the Middle Ages, although their diagrams do not survive. Medieval engineers developed cranks, waterwheels, clockworks, and pumps to build a civilization based on mechanical power rather than on the labor of slaves.

The builders of monuments during the early modern era took up the techniques of perspective drawing advanced by

Alberti and others. Renaissance engineers kept notebooks with drawings, of which Leonardo da Vinci's are the best known. The diagrams found in his notebooks are of several types: *time-motion* diagrams showing processes one phase at a time, *details* magnifying important or complex areas, *exploded views* displaying parts disassembled in order, *cross-sections* slicing through a whole, *cutaways* removing the external layer, and *phantom views* making the exterior skin transparent, all to expose the inner parts and workings of things. Da Vinci did not invent these types of diagrams but benefitted from the engineering tradition.

Like many of da Vinci's diagrams, the drawings of Gaspard Monge from the late eighteenth and early nineteenth centuries dealt with military machinery. His descriptive geometry sped up the building of military fortifications and contributed to the methods still used in diagrams. But not until the spread of the blueprint process, late in the nineteenth century, did the conventions of technical drawing become relatively fixed or standardized.

The Modern Forms: Tables and Graphs

Although making lists may be as ancient as mapping and diagramming, extensive tabulation appears to be an early modern invention. The history of tables has largely fallen under the purview of accounting. Besides several single-volume histories (e.g., Chatfield; Have; Littleton), there are also historical studies of specific accounting techniques (e.g., Snell; Radicati). According to these histories, the ancestors of tabulation were circular calendars and trade narratives.

Early calendars appeared when civilizations first arrayed their astronomical observations in circular form. Circle calendars of solar and lunar motions helped priests and temple cults direct planting and the harvest. Mesoamerican calendars are not clearly understood, but the Sumerian calendar divided

FIGURE 3.4.
Tabulation as
narrative.
Silver balanced
account, Ur
III, c. 2000
B.C.E. Pl. xv in
*Ledgers and
Prices: Early
Mesopotamian
Merchant
Accounts*, by
Daniel C.
Snell (New
Haven: Yale
UP, 1982).

the year into 360 days. The Egyptians increased the accuracy of the calendar, and by 700 B.C.E., the Assyrians had assembled some of the earliest surviving relational arrays, which compare the lunar and solar years.

Like calendars, tax and trade records also combined written language with numbers. The earliest Babylonian (Figure 3.4) and Egyptian transactions were usually recorded as stories, although they maintained some lists of commodities received and disbursed. Such records became regular reports tied to the lunar calendar in China during the Chao dynasty, which lasted from 1122 to 256 B.C.E. The Greeks continued to record commodity trade as simple barter stories even after they began issuing standardized coins around 630 B.C.E. The government sometimes disclosed public finances by chiseling accounts onto a marble pillar. Although Rome had a centralized system of coinage, taxes, and administrative records, and Roman households had bookkeeping and bank accounts, their records continued to be narrative in form. One reason tabulation did not emerge from the Romans is that their numerals for tens, hundreds, and other values do not line up consistently in a vertical list of numbers.

Place value, the assigning of a specific position to quantities of certain magnitudes, emerged slowly elsewhere. In England, sheriffs under William the Conqueror marked taxes paid on a tally stick. Notches the width of the palm, thumb,

FIGURE 3.5.
Place value in
Inca *quipu*
string
accounts.
Felipe
Guamán Poma
de Ayala,
*Nueva Crónica
y Buen
Gobierno*, 1613
(Paris: Institut
d'Ethnologie,
U Paris, 1936)
360.

and little finger indicated a thousand, a hundred, and twenty pounds, respectively. By splitting the notched stick lengthwise, each party could retain a copy, identified by engraving along the flat side. This record was brought to an annual "audit," or hearing, conducted around a table divided into squares. The auditors arranged a rank of credit markers (corresponding to the amounts paid, shown on the notches of the tally stick) alongside the rank of debit markers (for the taxes due), to discover the balance owing. This table gave rise to the term *exchequer* and to the checkerboard. In the Andes, the Incas recorded transactions by tying knots in a set of strings called *quipus* (Figure 3.5). Different knots acted as numbers in a decimal system, and their position along the strings indicated place value.

After the Crusades ended in the thirteenth century, increasing trade and credit pushed bankers and merchants to combine prose with place-value systems. These were bona fide tables, unlike the narratives and simple lists used earlier. Modern tables array accounts in two dimensions, so that the precise vertical and horizontal position determines what each number stands for. The Italian city-states codified accounting tabulation, which was later described in the 1494 textbook by Luca Pacioli. What came to be called the "method of Venice" established the standard in Europe until the nineteenth century. Early accountants preferred Roman numerals, which cannot be easily altered. The diffusion of Arabic numerals encouraged a vertical organization of space, facilitating the addition of columns, and leading to tables with many cells (or in recent jargon, *data points*).

The most recent chart form to be developed is the graph. The history of graphs has been the province of several fields, including business and commerce, economics, engineering, and statistics (Funkhouser). General handbooks for graph making began to appear in the United States in the early twentieth century (e.g., Arkin and Colton), and recent books on the subject have been published specifically for journalists (e.g., Holmes, *Designer's;* Sullivan; Wildbur). Many of these works outline the history of graphs.

Historians date graphing from the late fourteenth century, when several mathematicians, including Nicole d'Oresme, used graphs to demonstrate proofs (Figure 3.6). Da Vinci's notebooks contain several types of graphs as proofs, including one, for instance, that demonstrates that the speed of falling objects is constant. According to tradition, graphing ideas were considerably strengthened by René Descartes, who sug-

FIGURE 3.6. Graphs as a form of proof. Nicole d'Oresme, *Tractatus de configurationibus qualitatum et motuum,* 1382, trans. Marshall Clagett (Madison: U of Wisconsin P, 1968) pl. 7 (ms. from Groningen, Bibl. der Rijksuniv., 103, 69v. 16c).

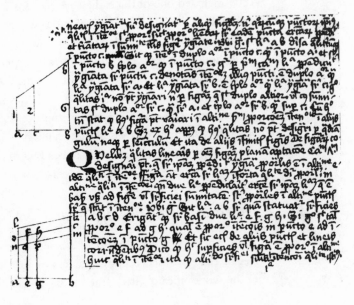

gested in a footnote to a philosophical treatise in 1637 that a grid on a two-dimensional surface can precisely plot the relationship between two numbers. These coordinates result from two scales, the horizontal abscissa, or x-axis, and the vertical ordinate, or y-axis. Descartes's analytical geometry established the pattern for displaying mathematical equations in two dimensions. The Cartesian grid forms the basis of many types of graphs.

By the mid-1700s, works on graphing techniques began to appear, and a quantity of books demonstrating statistical graphs was published by late in the same century. The best known of these is a book of financial statistics containing graphs on British trade published by William Playfair in 1786. Playfair had been educated by his brother, a mathematician at the University of Edinburgh, and had learned technical drafting at an engineering firm in England. With these skills, he perfected the *line graph*, which plots changes in measurements such as commodities or money over time, and the *bar graph*, which compares distinct activities (such as imports and exports) by a shared measurement such as number or value. The statistical atlas of the United States that he published in 1805 included one of the earliest *pie graphs*, which show a circular whole divided proportionally into wedged parts.

Graphing since Playfair has continued to elaborate these forms while adding others. The use of linear perspective allows the depiction of a third dimension of data. In the 1930s, statisticians working with trade and census data in Germany developed a system of using icons instead of bars. Perspective and illustration can accommodate more data sets in a graph but have been the subject of ongoing controversies (to be described later in this chapter).

Historical Meanings of Charts

Space does not allow more than a brief outline of the histories of charts, which occupy chapters or span entire volumes in the works already cited. But a gloss on each history at least suggests some roots of meaning common to graphic forms, which have been outlined by scholars (e.g., Mukerji). For example, charts clearly did not arise from domestic concerns or rites of love and courtship. Their invention did not result from leisure, entertainment, or sport. Instead, they originated in the service of commerce and wealth and in the pursuit of military action. They were also products of machine culture, acting as the tools of technological change.

Maps and tables are most closely associated with business and commerce in these histories. Accounting narratives, lists, and tables created records needed to separate ownership from possession. Greater wealth than one person or group could physically control was amassed by placing property in the hands of managers, who were prevented from turning possession into ownership because of a system of accounting. Temples and kings of antiquity kept lists of transactions and inventories to control property and prevent fraud.

Ancient traders not only depended on tables or accounts but also required a knowledge of trade routes. Whether something got mapped and listed depended largely on its commercial value. The river of gold running through central Africa on early maps clearly signals their function as guides to wealth. Maps have only recently become an adjunct to travel for purposes other than trade. Like tables, maps originated as instruments of economic power, extending the reach of commerce beyond the realm of the individual.

In these histories, maps and diagrams are the forms most closely tied to the military. Cartography, especially, is connected with the history of empire building centered in Europe. Roman roads facilitated commerce but served primarily for the movement and supply lines of the imperial legions. Cartography itself became one of the spoils of conquest when Europeans absorbed the mapmaking traditions of the cultures they colonized. Europe came to occupy the strategic center of cartography, with other places and societies on the periphery.

An early motivation for making diagrams was to expedite the engineering required for battle. Many of da Vinci's diagrams described machines for defensive warfare as well as for attack. The pattern of diagramming for war continued with Monge, whose work was kept a military secret for thirty years before being published in 1795. Diagrams used for combat have long been the link between military advantage and technology.

Technology is an explicit focus of the histories of maps, diagrams, and tables. The influence of technique is felt in two ways, in the causes and in the consequences of these visual forms. The mechanisms used to gather and present information help determine what forms charts eventually take, and so technology is thought to cause or to affect the graphic forms themselves. But the forms also convey assumptions that help define reality, and, as a consequence, technology may indirectly influence how the world is defined and seen.

Technology as a cause of visual form emerges most clearly in the history of maps. When the Académie Royale des

FIGURE 3.7. Maps and reality. (The lighter outline represents the older version of the coastline.) *Carte de France corrigée par ordre du Roy sur les observations de Mrs de l'Académie des Sciences,* engraving, 1693, 1:4,120,000 (36.0 x 26.6 cm, Bibliothèque Nationale, Paris, no. Ge. DD 2987-777). Rpt. in *Cartography in France 1660–1848: Science, Engineering, and Statecraft,* by Josef W. Konvitz (Chicago: U of Chicago P, 1987) 8.

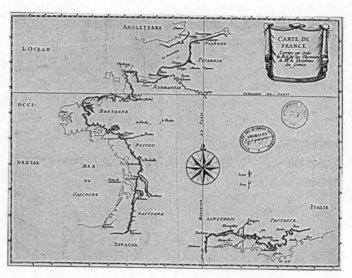

Sciences used the surveying technique called triangulation to pinpoint the location of the coastline of France, Louis XIV found his realm considerably shrunk (Figure 3.7). The map itself had changed. Besides surveying instruments, other technical tools and methods each in turn reshaped maps: the mariner's compass, the quadrant and the astrolabe, aerial photography, digital computers, and the like. By increasing the precision of measurements, technology enhanced the authority of maps, as well as changing the appearance of the things mapped.

The consequences of how things look can be best illustrated from the history of diagrams. Since ancient times, diagrams have described the pulleys, cranks, and ropes of machine technology. Diagrams developed not only to show the visual appearance of things but also to identify their parts, show how they are put together, and explain how they function or operate. The histories of engineering suggest that this mechanistic way of thinking eventually became a central metaphor in the Middle Ages. Behind the external surfaces of things, the internal, often invisible reality was thought to be made of parts that fit together to serve some purpose.

As the machine metaphor permeated medieval thought, mechanical devices flowered (Figure 3.8). Engineering historians see the period not as a dark age but as a time of steady technical advances, such as those inspired by the invention of clockworks. The diagram of the mechanism seems to reveal the reality, so that behind the face and sweeping hands of the clock, for example, time itself seems to be driven by mechanical clockworks. The machine metaphor came to equate all sorts of human and social action with mechanical devices that direct natural forces to produce change. One consequence of diagramming techniques is that their visual forms come to influence the perception of how the world works.

A further example can be found in the tables invented during the Renaissance. From early narrative accounts that combined words and chronology to tell the story of commercial

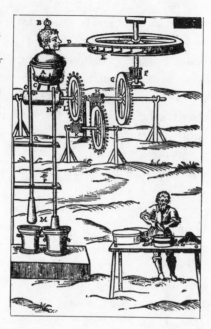

FIGURE 3.8.
Diagrams as
ideas.
*Conception of
Steam Turbine,*
Branca, *La
Macchine*
(1629). Fig.
6.10 in Kirby
et al. 152.

transactions, tabulation evolved a structure based on mechanistic thinking. Tables function as input and output, so that each item in the list has a corresponding entry in each category, that is, each cause has related effects. In this sense, tables are the graphic apotheosis of a mechanical ideal.

⚅ Tables embody human imagination, just as other graphic forms do. Maps and tables make a mental concept concrete by extending ownership to things beyond the physical control of one individual. Diagrams, as well as maps, distill ideas that may contribute to military victory or repel the invader. All of these forms, even when used to serve other purposes, continue to reflect these historical assumptions about human beings, property, and machines in society. Charts in newspapers can thus be read not only as information but also as evidence of a culture's beliefs and values.

*P*ower and Graphic Correspondence

Through their roles in economics, the military, and technology, charts have helped impose social order and consolidate political power. The histories of the forms indicate three ways that charts work visually to establish power in society: by plotting the center of control, by showing lines of authority, and by asserting balance and equilibrium. These means depend on a notion central to all chart making: that there can be a one-to-one correspondence between the measurements of the real world and their graphic representation.

Maps have played an important role in plotting the center of power. The Greeks placed the prime meridian in Delphi. In ancient Eastern maps, China and Japan occupy the center. The roads of Roman maps radiated from the hub of Rome. Many medieval maps placed Jerusalem at the center and east at the top, but that orientation eventually changed, putting Europe on top and at the center. One of the principal functions of maps, to place the unknown in relation to the known, required that French maps start from France and that, later, English maps begin from England. This tradition might be added to the list of necessary white lies described by Mark Monmonier in *How to Lie with Maps*. What is known depends on one point of view — that of the individuals and groups in power. Monmonier documents many cases of groups' creating maps to make their particular interests central (*Lie*).

Cartographers usually draw a distinction between general *base maps*, which primarily indicate locations, and *thematic maps*, which use base maps as a foundation for complex combinations with other data. These two forms are commonly called *locator maps* and *data maps* in newspaper parlance. Recent cartographic scholarship asserts that the political and economic boundaries and locations inscribed in base maps are not neutral data but representations of power (e.g., Harley; Wood and Fels). The cartographer Denis Wood suggests shedding the pretense of neutral objectivity, which can make geography seem dull, and acknowledging the subjective stories maps and atlases tell. Thematic maps compound subjectivity by superimposing on base maps a set of data selected from a point of view, with its assumptions about what is worth measuring by what scale.

Diagrams have played an important role in showing lines of authority. Early civilizations used diagrams as a tool for building monuments. The diagrams themselves made abstract

FIGURE 3.9. Diagrams and lines of authority. Moving a heavy statue, bas relief in a tomb, Nineveh. From Kirby et al. 17.

ideas, such as the division of labor for complex or large human endeavors, seem concrete. An Assyrian tomb drawing of a statue being moved (Figure 3.9) illustrates the role of diagrams as tools for and conduits of ideas. The diagram reveals the value assigned to feats involving size and to the imagery of statuary. Its form is also an artifact of political ideas, suggesting a hierarchical system of power and control. The highly conventionalized diagramming may seem to be a neutral report of events or a set of instructions, but it also allows those who control its form to reiterate their power and to influence ideas about themselves and their subordinates. Ferguson argues that during the nineteenth century the emergence of standardized technical drawing shifted power from skilled craftsmen to managers who controlled the drafting room. Drawing became the instrument of authority.

Tables have played a role in asserting political equilibrium. The tabulations of early modern Italy transformed the narrative accounts of the ancient Mediterranean world into a regular system for creating an ordered totality out of inchoate human relations. A belief in stability is desirable for those who wish to sustain the existing structure of power. Tables use visual position to create evidence for a world of stable balance, where each debit has a corresponding credit, and for a world of uniformity, where each entry has the same potential data points. A doctrine of uniformity projects the status quo onto the past and into the future, enhancing the position of those already in power.

All of these chart forms developed and have continued to be employed to support stable central authority. To do so they depend on the common belief in graphic correspondence, the notion that numbers (measurements such as time and distance) can be accurately represented by increments of ink and space on a two-dimensional surface. The earliest maps and plans of Mesopotamia demonstrate a belief in one-to-one correspondence between markings and physical objects. Evidence for the faith in this parallel between reality and its representations can also be found in the practice of drawing to scale.

Some conformity between the display and the reality is a practical necessity for communication to occur. Charts become more useful as the forms become standard. Reducing the variation in the mode of display to a minimum makes the information more widely intelligible. When Playfair presented his early bar graphs, he had to explain that the x-axis showed the passage of time and the length of the bars represented quantities of goods. Convention since then has rendered such elaborations unnecessary. The time line now almost always goes on the bottom, from left to right. The practical utility of standard forms is an important virtue of all forms of communication.

One problem, once standards have emerged, is that graphic forms begin to seem whole, as if they fully represented some facet of the natural world. A pie graph does not pretend to show more than a part of reality, but that part seems complete in form. Despite the ease of accepting the familiar pie graph as objective, an irreducible minimum of variability always remains — a fudge factor that allows subjective judgments to enter in. The size of the pie, the shading of the wedges, their positions around the circle, and many other visual effects give off rhetorical signals. That variability is difficult to hold in mind.

A rhetorical quality permeates all graphic forms, regardless of how rigorous a standard they follow. Playfair experimented with graphs that used the size of the circle to show the magnitude of the data. Circle graphs are often condemned as hard to read precisely, but pie pieces are no more exact. Neither form uses the Cartesian grid. In the common bar graph, only one axis contains a scale. The other determines the widths of bars, an important factor that can be used to make the data seem substantial or lightweight. But the line graph built on Cartesian coordinates also admits variation, in the scale, shading, weight of lines, and other graphic effects.

Eliminating all variation not only is impossible but would also be undesirable. The rhetoric of charts accommodates the human need to read subjective intent, to see which way the wind is blowing. A chart can look neutral only by disguising its author's purpose, which may serve to make it dishonest as well as dull. Graphic variability also fulfills a human desire for variety. Line graphs may seem monotonous precisely because the grids of pie and bar graphs are not as controlling. But any form, too often used, can become a bore.

The principle of graphic correspondence is present in maps, diagrams, and tables, as well as graphs. As a practical matter, diagrams must conform to real details for communication to occur. But that correspondence masks a view of nature as a machinelike clockwork. Tables also seem to present transactions whole, although they substitute a regular grid for the idiosyncratic narratives of social interaction. Even the common map, with its rigorous standard projections, imposes political structures on the natural landscape. Graphs may seem to step away from nature, toward the monosemic or neutral realm of numbers, but they, too, assert the principle that marks on paper can correspond to reality. Much of the power of these graphic forms to reinforce the existing social and political order springs from the underlying authority of numbers and statistics.

S ocial Measurement in History

Numbers themselves are neutral only in the ideal. Even as abstractions, they may come laden with social meanings, magical properties, and superstitions. But numbers rarely crop up in everyday life as abstractions. Instead, they take part in the practical process of naming and defining objects and affairs in society. The meanings of numbers in culture have played a central role in the emergence of the social sciences (Lécuyer and Oberschall). Modern statistics has resulted as much from the cultural meanings of numbers as from the mathematics that usually takes the spotlight in histories of the subject (Stigler; Porter). The study of the rising socially expected level of numerical knowledge, called *numeracy*, forms a growing field in the history of ideas (e.g., Cohen; Alonzo; Herbst). An overview of statistics and numeracy in history can expose additional root meanings of the charts in newspapers.

Modern interest in measuring human society began in the seventeenth century in response to social disarray. Events such as the Great Plague of 1665 and the Thirty Years' War in Europe disrupted the old system based on class distinctions and characterizations. In England, taking a census was seen as a way to somehow put back in place the growing numbers of dislocated homeless in the city and vagabonds in the country-side. These problems coincided with the expansion of trade and the development of insurance, which also required accounts of people and goods. Private enthusiasts undertook the earliest research on social phenomena to uncover large-scale regularity in human affairs. One English study divided the population into twenty-four strata, from lords to vagrants.

Numbering and measuring society held the promise of a new political order. Population was thought to produce national wealth, and the size of principal cities became a source of national pride. Good government, it seemed, might yet be built on a foundation of precise information. These

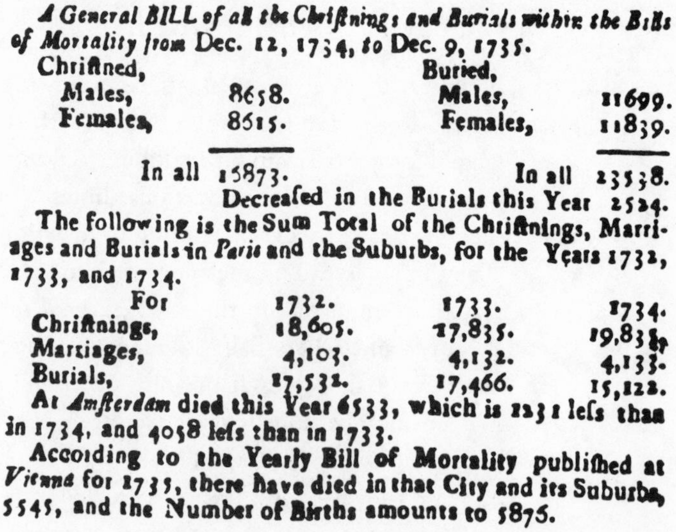

FIGURE 3.10.
Early chart
from an
American
newspaper.
"Bills of
Mortality,"
*Boston Evening
Post* 10 May
1736 (micro-
form, Bird
Library,
Syracuse
University).

A General BILL of all the Chriftnings and Burials within the Bills of Mortality from Dec. 12, 1734, *to* Dec. 9, 1735.

Chriftned,		Buried,	
Males,	8658.	Males,	11699.
Females,	8515.	Females,	11839.

In all 15873.   In all 23538.
Decreafed in the Burials this Year 2524.

The following is the Sum Total of the Chriftnings, Marriages and Burials in *Paris* and the Suburbs, for the Years 1732, 1733, and 1734.

	1732.	1733.	1734.
For Chriftnings,	18,605.	17,835.	19,835.
Marriages,	4,103.	4,132.	4,133.
Burials,	17,531.	17,466.	15,122.

At *Amfterdam* died this Year 6533, which is 1231 lefs than in 1734, and 4058 lefs than in 1733.

According to the Yearly Bill of Mortality publifhed at *Vienna* for 1735, there have died in that City and its Suburbs, 5545, and the Number of Births amounts to 5875.

ideas spread in the eighteenth century, and newspapers began to publish articles discussing population changes. In the United States, demographic lists appeared with the *Boston News Letter* as "Bills of Mortality," a form adopted from English papers (Figure 3.10).

The new political order depended not only on precise enumerations but also on a citizenry capable of understanding them. Eighteenth-century newspapers began running articles extolling the practical and universal benefits of numerical skills. In the United States, Thomas Jefferson and Noah Webster, among others, argued that democracy required training the rational minds of all citizens. By the early nineteenth century, numeracy became accepted as a requisite skill of citizenship and as a desirable intellectual attribute. Alexis de Tocqueville noted the enthusiasm for detailed calculations in Jacksonian America. The founding of the public-school system and the growth of a market economy helped increase the interest in mental arithmetic.

Improvements in the citizenry could in turn be measured regularly by governments. The nineteenth century saw the institution of decennial censuses in Britain and the United

States. When enthusiasm for government statistics and individual betterment converged with the social upheavals from industrialization, reform movements took hold in Europe and the United States. Problems such as poverty, the lack of education and sanitation, and the conditions in prisons, workplaces, and housing led European reformers to propose changes in schools, government, health care, and other institutions.

In the United States, the first censuses revealed not an egalitarian society but one divided by class and wealth. Clerics, politicians, merchants, and others used statistics to define some social issues as important. The problems they identified, such as prostitution and drunkenness, were seen as solvable, the result of poor hygiene or inadequate schooling. This view of causes and effects determined the course of social statistics. Questions were added to the U.S. census as new problems emerged (Alonzo). When immigration came to be seen as a problem, for example, census-takers began to ask people to specify their country of origin.

In Britain, a much-admired study by the demographer Charles Booth in the 1880s set out to show well-heeled

FIGURE 3.11. Charts and social divisions. Charles Booth, *Descriptive Map of London Poverty 1889* (British Museum, Cat. no. 08275.bb.5).

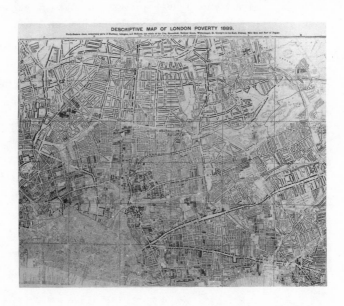

London how the other half lived. Booth eventually divided families into eight classes according to income and tied class to geography by color-coding neighborhoods block by block (Figure 3.11). The massive study contributed to the enactment of provisions for pensions, minimum wages, disability, and unemployment and was widely imitated in other countries. Besides their positive effects, these studies also served to reinforce the segregation of social classes, defining those with lower incomes as the clients or beneficiaries of the upper classes.

By the end of the century, the benign view that society's problems are solvable was widely replaced by social Darwinism. The programs of reformers were reinterpreted as a danger to natural selection, because they aided the weak, thereby weakening the fiber of society. Studies began to emphasize race and heredity, which became identified as the causes of crime and other social evils. Researchers thought that heredity and impairments had produced inferior species of humans, which could be classified by their physical characteristics, such as the dimensions of the skull. Played on a background of post–Civil War America, social Darwinism had the effect of replacing slavery with a newly powerful set of social-scientific divisions.

From their origins in the seventeenth century, social statistics and numeracy have helped to establish and consolidate authority. The measurements originated as a response to social disorder, but the new order amassed power in the hands of the numerate, who set out to cure society's ills. Numbers cannot provide a dispassionate measure of social evils because no definition of evil can be dispassionate. Thus the laudable reforms to improve the conditions of daily life also worked to reinforce the superiority of those with the power to define the problems. Social Darwinism, although subsequently discredited, provides yet another example of statistical measurements that serve political power by creating or emphasizing social categories and divisions. This tendency has continued in the twentieth century with the emergence of surveys on public attitudes and opinions.

Reading Newspaper Charts

N ewspaper charts, in turn, have inherited the political and social proclivities of statistics and numeracy. Even the charts in your local paper may reinforce patterns of power and dominance by defining the problems of certain classes and also by conveying the neutral authority of the charts themselves. They may also convey the vestiges of historical chart making described earlier, with ties to business and commerce, the military, and technology. These possibilities make good candidates for the enumerating and classifying methods of quantitative study. To explore the meanings behind current uses of charts in journalism, this exercise will walk you through your own informal study of the charts in your newspaper.

You should perform this exercise less for academic than for practical benefits. The experience demonstrates the value of empirical investigation. Your study won't by itself prove, but will instead engage you in, the argument that looking beyond the surface of newspaper charts is an indispensable skill for editors and critical readers. The experience also reveals the subjective side of quantitative research. Your study will confront you firsthand with the many judgments all researchers must make. Finally, the experience juxtaposes quantitative with impressionistic exploration. Your informal study will bring into contrast the relative authority of quantitative analysis and qualitative work.

You will need a large collection of charts from the newspaper you ordinarily read. First, simply count up the charts. You don't have to clip them all, but at least mark their locations for later reference. Some metropolitan dailies publish many charts in a single daily edition, and you can use them all. One Sunday paper alone might be sufficient. If your newspaper publishes only a few charts each day, use a full week's output or save enough issues to collect no fewer than twenty charts. A larger sample, of course, has a better chance of revealing patterns. Round numbers make computing easier. In a group of one hundred, for example, every chart is also a percentage point. But too big a group becomes a practical burden without revealing much more than does a group of manageable size. Decide for yourself how large a population of charts to collect.

Counting charts raises another challenge. Any system of counting involves choices of what to include or exclude. What exactly qualifies as a chart? Maps and diagrams are easy to spot, as are most graphs, but tables blur the distinction between writing and charting. Simple lists may not present a clear-cut choice. Would you include recipes from the food page? What about bulleted items in the middle of news stories? Are classified ads a tabulation? Counting is also more variable than it seems at first. Business and sports pages, for instance, report results in classic table style, with multiple cells. But does each market and game constitute a separate table? Look at the charts, make a practical judgment, and count them up. You will review your solution to these problems later.

Once you have collected a generous, round number of charts, classify them. Systems of classification spring from the questions being asked. Dividing the sample into maps, diagrams, tables, and graphs would answer some questions of description but wouldn't get at the historical connections. Instead, you might label each chart for any ties to business, the military, and technology. These categories will probably overlap. A graph of computer sales, for example, falls under two or possibly all three categories. Classifying also requires many judgments. The categories can be defined narrowly or broadly, so that the term *military* might be limited to direct references to armed forces or expanded to the theme of conflict. Outside of results statistics, charts on the sports page may be illustrated or presented as metaphors for military battles or for economic competition. Watch for these connections, but be evenhanded as you classify each chart. As you work, be open to other themes and include them in your classifications.

Your data so far should include the total number of charts and the number within each classification. If you didn't keep a tally while classifying the charts, take a few minutes now to count how many fall into each category. Then compare that number with the total (that is, divide each category by the total). The resulting figure is a percentage that indicates the share of charts with military, commercial, and technological ties. Also compute the shares for any other categories that emerged as you worked.

Study the percentages to see how your judgments may have affected the outcome. If you worked from a small population, for example, each chart has a greater effect on the resulting shares. Your decisions about what to count can shift the data as well. If you considered each team's results as a separate table, then the sports section might dominate the data. Formal studies in academic journals must account for these decisions by giving precise definitions and describing methods clearly. Aside from making for dry reading, strict protocols provide some assurance that a fair-minded person repeating the study would come up with similar results. After reaching this point, consider how you would change your counting and classifying decisions if you were to start again.

A more difficult task is to make sense of the results. The percentages give the impression of precision and authority. But just what do those numbers mean? Is the share of business, military, or technical charts "high" or "low"? How large must a vestige of influence from history be to take on significance? A "vestige" has no exact cutoff point and may in fact be quite small. You must determine whether any ties you discovered are weak or strong. What does the evidence say to you? Could other reasonable people interpret the results very differently? Your purpose is not to prove anything but to think deliberately about the charts themselves and about the difficulty of counting and measuring.

As you consider, return to the charts to look for the workings of power. This time you can explore qualitatively, without keeping a precise tally. Begin by trying to discover who is the "we" or "us" speaking through each chart. Study any sources listed to find out who controlled the research. Were the data from a governmental body or census or from a private research group? What are the researchers' politics? Also study any credits given for the chart design. Was the work done locally or by a national syndicate? The two perspectives make a difference in whether the data approximate the experience in your community. A local design may define what matters differently from a national design. As you look through the charts again, make notes about who is given authority and who has a right to speak through the newspaper's charts.

Next, try to discover who is on the other side, the "they" or "them" being described through the charts. Study any data to find out who is the object of research and what groups are candidates for reform or need fixing. Besides verbal clues, look for purely visual forms of emphasis. Sometimes "they" are identified by differentiating and emphasizing their bar, line, or piece of pie. "They" might be shown as darker or more brightly colored, on a dramatically different scale, or as seeming to pop out from the background. Also look for problems. What are the social evils or ills needing remedy? How do they relate to the definitions of "us" and "them," of who has power and who needs mending?

Some charts may also carry a subtle social agenda. Do any of them propose to have found natural limitations of the client groups? They probably will not espouse social Darwinism but may point to nature, perhaps in genetics or biology, as a deterministic cause of social phenomena. Do any of them propose to have found curable causes for social problems? Many charts may succeed in being neutral on these issues. Be sure to examine any accompanying pictures or illustrations for subtle cues, because the assumptions may not be explicit in the words. Jot down your observations.

From this impressionistic look at the qualities of charts, draw some conclusions about power. What role did government play?

How about outside groups? Was the perspective national or local? Who is in charge, and who has the problems? What sorts of problems did the charts define? Were they considered solvable or embedded in nature? As you list your observations, indicate how confident you are in each of them.

Finally, compare the experiences of quantitative and qualitative study. Was one approach more satisfying than the other? Counting and classifying may seem much more concrete, specific, and reliable. Did you have that impression? Gathering impressions may seem amorphous and arbitrary. Did you suppress any urge to quantify? There are probably many ways that your impressions could be backed up with numbers or your counting enhanced by qualitative observations. Enumerating can provide insights obscured to the qualitative observer or contrary to received opinion. Both approaches, like all human endeavors, are subjectively based. Your reactions to each process may spring from your acculturation as well as from a personal preference for numbers or impressionistic work. Either method must be judged by the value of the insights it provides. Were you startled by anything you found? Did you see from a perspective you don't usually take? Were your expectations contradicted?

To prepare for what follows, make a quick sketch of how you would display the results of your study. The presentation need not be elaborate. You might try to imitate the charts from the newspaper you studied. Which would get the bigger play, the quantitative or impressionistic results? Think about the forms you might use. The numbers would fit into a graph of some sort, but the impressions probably would not. Both might be turned into a list. These concerns about the practical construction of charts have been the primary focus of some scholarly media research.

Efficient and Vivid Charts

In the late 1980s, numerous articles in the trade press and academic journals documented the rising use of charts in newspapers (e.g., Cvengros; Hilliard; Terrell). Along with anecdotal evidence, these articles quantified the changes. Content studies counted the charts appearing in newspapers, and surveys measured editors' attitudes toward charts and their use of in-house equipment and graphics distribution networks. Book-length studies also appeared (Monmonier, *Maps;* Holmes, *Pictorial*). These descriptive works clearly document the widespread enthusiasm for charts in newspaper journalism.

The authors and their survey respondents tend to see charts as an efficient alternative to text, made possible by personal computers. They also express the hope that charts will attract readers and buttress circulation. The measures of the enthusiasm for charts often get interpreted as causes of their spread. Computerization seems to make charts practical, competitive marketing to make them a necessity. Although the technology and the circulation concerns have emerged simultaneously, they do not necessarily increase chart use. They do, however, extend the long connection between charts and commerce and technology.

> $\mathcal{N}$ews is
> anything that
> makes a
> reader say,
> "Gee whiz!"
>
> — *Arthur McEwen*

The reason scholars, editors, and designers most frequently cite for their enthusiasm is that charts are useful and attractive to readers. These ideas — functional utility and persuasive appeal — are central to both popular and scholarly theory about charts. Besides descriptive studies, the field has spawned dozens of quantitative studies in psychology, education, and communications (summarized in Kosslyn; Macdonald-Ross; David). These articles share their concern for efficiency and attractiveness with the various how-to manuals (e.g., Schmid; Sullivan). Charts are also the subject of theories developed in psychology (Cleveland) and semiotics (Bertin). Some studies also evaluate the ability of readers to use and understand charts (e.g., Pasternack and Utt).

The functional utility of charts is central to all the experimental research surrounding their use. The studies are of two varieties. One strain seeks to clarify how charts work in the context of words on the page. The experiments often compare reading text alone with viewing a combination of chart and text. Most authors believe charts are more efficient than text, especially for presenting large quantities of information. So far, experiments using pencil-and-paper tests to measure recall have produced mixed results. Critics point out that the tests may measure reading skills and short-term memory rather than any effects of graphic or textual form.

The other strain in the research compares the relative efficiency of various charts. Readers encountering the same information in a table and a graph, for instance, are tested for rapid and correct responses. Once again, the results are mixed. The studies do not consistently show one graphic form to be a faster or more accurately recalled mode of display than another. Some computer-based experiments precisely measure the time respondents take to answer questions while viewing charts. These studies improve on those that measure memory and reading skills, but the findings have yet to produce reliable rules for selecting chart forms.

Studies of how readers use and understand charts warn fairly consistently that charts present difficulties to all but the most sophisticated reader (e.g., Culbertson and Powers; Peel; Roller). Broad-based tests of literacy suggest that only a minority of the U.S. population can successfully interpret charts (e.g., Egan; National Assessment). One extensive study of a specific chart, the "food pyramid" developed for the U.S. Department of Agriculture (Figure 3.12), found that the difficulty extends even to well-educated readers ("Executive Summary"). By these measures, charts in newspapers may not have much functional utility for many readers.

Experimental researchers speculate that charts are more attractive than text even if they don't streamline information. But the persuasive appeal of charts, so often mentioned in

FIGURE 3.12.
Chart that may
be difficult to
interpret. Bell
Associates, for
the U.S.
Department of
Agriculture,
1992.

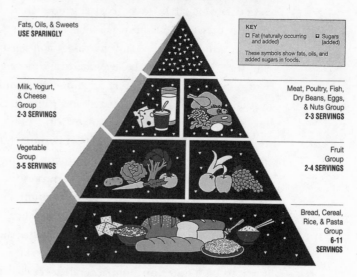

Food Guide Pyramid
A Guide to Daily Food Choices

KEY
☐ Fat (naturally occurring   ☑ Sugars
and added)   (added)
These symbols show fats, oils, and
added sugars in foods.

Fats, Oils, & Sweets
USE SPARINGLY

Milk, Yogurt,
& Cheese
Group
2-3 SERVINGS

Meat, Poultry, Fish,
Dry Beans, Eggs,
& Nuts Group
2-3 SERVINGS

Vegetable
Group
3-5 SERVINGS

Fruit
Group
2-4 SERVINGS

Bread, Cereal,
Rice, & Pasta
Group
6-11
SERVINGS

popular articles and descriptive surveys, has been little studied. Theoreticians have proposed that readers process charts
differently from text. Working from cognitive psychology,
they hypothesize that charts are encoded as visual images.
These might allow the mind to refer to charts as a sort of vir-
tual reality, with their dimensional quality intact. Multiple
dimensions may encourage dynamic comparisons (the spot-
ting of trends and patterns that would be obscured in text).
The images may also make recall much stronger. But robust
research findings have yet to confirm these theories. Improved
dynamic comparisons do show up in some experiments, but
stronger recall of charts and graphs has not turned up consistently.

Although charts are not singled out, an extensive literature
in psychology (summarized by Taylor and Thompson; Collins
et al.) explores the popular belief that some forms of communication are more vivid than others. The belief in vividness
extends to many fields. Writers consider concrete language

more vivid than abstractions. Teachers think their lessons are stronger with visual aids such as pictures and videos than without. Business managers and professionals think that direct action outperforms vicarious experience and that case studies surpass "dry" statistical information. In all these forms, vividness is supposed to achieve an emotional impact by provoking mental imagery.

In dozens of studies, researchers generated very little empirical evidence for the existence of vividness, but they did show that people *believe* the effect exists. Social psychologists, marketing experts, advertisers, and presumably journalists work from the theory that the vividness of their communications has an influence on other people but not on themselves. Study participants who have no special expertise also share the belief that other people are subject to a vividness effect to which they themselves are immune. Although vividness may be illusory, the widespread belief in its effect has fed the enthusiasm for chart making.

If some great catastrophe is not announced every morning, we feel a certain void. "Nothing in the paper today," we sigh.

— *Paul Valéry*

◙ Common beliefs about charts have influenced the record of history, scholarship, and practice. Many articles and studies cite the belief that *USA Today* was the innovator in newspaper charts, although in fact other papers led the way. The belief in the practical utility of charts has led scholars to continue searching for the measures of efficiency. These beliefs, along with vividness, have encouraged newspaper publishers to buy computer technology and look to charts for some competitive advantage. Even without much backup from research, beliefs about innovativeness, usefulness, and attractiveness have helped increase the use of charts.

The Debate over Practice

Utility and vividness have also fueled an ongoing controversy among practitioners. Students of the field have traced the issues under debate to the eighteenth century (David), when Playfair sought to convey results and conclusions, while his contemporary J. H. Lambert used charts as a tool for analysis. Those who believe that vividness counts most argue that charts can be persuasive, supporting and illustrating a conclusion or point of view. Those committed to utility as an overriding value prefer that charts be informative, providing detailed data from which careful readers will extract whatever interests them.

Magazine designer Jan V. White, among others (e.g., Holmes, *Designer's*), proposes that charts be used vividly. Editors who expect articles to assume a particular angle or point of view, he argues, should expect charts to do the same. Putting a particular spin on events supplies the context for a story and reflects the journalist's judgment of what is right and good for society and for the reader. Everything about an article pushes for moral or political action—urging the reader to become an informed consumer or voter, for example—and charts should be no different. They should exercise a vivid, persuasive power.

In his studies *Envisioning Information* and *The Visual Display of Quantitative Information*, Professor Edward R. Tufte adopts the position that charts should be functionally useful. The conventions of chart making can remove any intentional bias, but only if they are applied assiduously. Illustrating charts and decorating the data usually serve only to confuse or distort the information. Simplifying by cutting back on data only makes charts boring. Although intended to be appealing, Tufte argues, simplified, decorative charts in fact insult the intelligence of readers. Charts become memorable and interesting not by their simple data and entertaining form but by their rich and detailed array of information that connects directly with many readers.

In the trade journals and the experimental studies described earlier, this debate between vivid persuasion and useful information has focused on specific practical questions. Should charts display data in the form of figurative drawings? Should designers employ linear perspective to enliven information? How should the proportions of the grid be chosen? On these and other questions, when the vivid persuaders take one position, the useful informants usually take the opposite.

Nobody's interested in sweetness and light.

— Hedda Hopper

⊠ Linear perspective gives an illusory depth to flat surfaces. But if the data are shown in the receding lines of perspective, some data points shrink compared with others. When bar graphs are rendered to look like blocks, the perspective lines, space, and shading reduce the visual differences between individual bars. Likewise, a pie graph tipped into perspective takes on an elliptical shape that enlarges the pieces in the front compared to those behind. The useful informants would argue that elliptical-pie and receding-bar graphs risk miscommunicating to the reader. The vivid persuaders would counter that flat graphs are boring and won't get read at all.

Figurative drawing gives a memorable physical form to the abstractions of statistics, tabulation, or cartography. But if the rectangular bars in a chart get turned into some other shape, they change size absolutely rather than proportionately. A short silo, for example, loses as much area in its rounded cap as a tall silo (or rocket, or stack of pennies) does. Making the silo wider as it gets taller changes everything in proportion, but it is difficult to compare area (two dimensions) rather than a single dimension such as height. A pie made to look like a human face will add features or appendages to some slices and not to others. The useful informants would object that the ink and space become unequal, that in effect only some slices get icing. The vivid persuaders would argue that a little inequality is better than no icing at all.

The most telling argument between these two groups concerns the proportions of the grid. The units used for most charts are not constant, as are inches and centimeters. With a grid that is much higher than it is wide, a line graph will display greater peaks and valleys than the same data would reveal on a broad, flat grid. A scale that doesn't begin at zero will also emphasize the range of variation. Changing the scale from, say, years to months makes the slope of the resulting line become more gradual. Given a chart with large empty spaces, vivid persuaders might lop off portions of the grid or fill in the gaps by changing the scale or perspective or by adding ornament. The useful informants might insist on keeping the space because it communicates part of the data, or they might use the space by adding more data.

These positions about perspective, illustrations, and the grid seem to deal with bedrock truth and accuracy. But charts are signs, not reality. They seem concrete because of the doctrine of graphic correspondence. Charts propose to represent the world first by measuring it and then by displaying those measurements in ink and space on paper. But decisions about display invariably confront absurdity: How many years are there in a printer's pica? How many racial minorities in a centimeter? How many deaths in an inch? These questions have no correct answer. Like language, a chart is a metaphor. Of course life is not paper and ink. Only imagination can make it so. Graphic artists, like writers, seek precision and vividness. These ideals are at odds with the muddled world, as well as with each other.

$\mathcal{E}$diting Charts

The standard textbooks on chart making attempt to guide practitioners through the muddle by setting standards (Nodley and Lowenstein; Rogers). On questions of accuracy, they echo the popular discussions of statistical ethics, such as Darrel Huff's classic *How to Lie with Statistics*, which show how the forms of charts can be manipulated (e.g., Monmonier, *Lie;* DeParle). The emerging industry standards also focus on two problems that editors can quickly identify: whether a chart is complete and appropriate.

Graphics editors have produced a variety of checklists for judging the completeness of charts. Usually, these depend on the customary parts and nomenclature. The *chart title* (not a headline) identifies the content and may hook the reader by wordplay. Next, a succinct line or paragraph called a *blurb* (or sometimes *chatter*) makes the chart self-explanatory. Toward the bottom, a *source line* tells where the data came from, and another line may credit the designer and reporter. The body of the chart includes the grid, data, and labels. Map projections and diagram perspectives are grids, although rarely identified in news. In graphs, the scale of the grid may be eliminated or replaced by labels for the quantities. Even for tables, custom dictates showing as little of the underlying grid as necessary. The data are considered complete when each point is present and labeled in parallel terms placed consistently near the data points.

The handbooks define charts as inappropriate when they have the wrong format for data. Traditionally, line or fever graphs plot changes over time, pie graphs show shares of a whole, and bar graphs compare distinct categories like apples and oranges. Maps present geographic data, and diagrams reveal physical appearance. Anything else belongs in a table. These distinctions lead to several rules of thumb for editors: Add up the parts of a pie graph to see if they make a whole.

In a line graph, check for consistent dates across the bottom. Question whether showing location is essential before approving a map. And so forth.

Standards and rules of thumb are valuable; they can help editors catch the most egregious errors. For example, polls of consumer preferences sometimes allow each respondent to choose several products. If the results are shown as a pie graph, what is the unitary whole? It doesn't correspond to the number of consumers, and the number of preferences chosen is too arbitrary to be a meaningful unit. Editors and critical readers should recognize that the pie graph is inappropriate for the data. However, following standards and rules of thumb does have its drawbacks. By checking for appropriateness, editors may insist on a few obvious chart types and discourage innovations that break the norm. Charts may then become routine or dull. Checking for completeness hardly addresses the question of what meanings a chart conveys.

🔯 Editors and critical readers can discover the meanings of charts by examining the data and the design in depth. Data emerge when researchers ask questions, define social groups, and take measurements. All of their procedures deserve close scrutiny. Designs emerge from graphic artists and their tools. The conditions under which they work require as much attention as the chart forms they produce. Decisions that lead to publishing a chart have an impact on individuals and social groups and are an expression of the values of journalists.

To evaluate the data, editors and critical readers must ask several probing questions. Who collected it for what purpose? How are social groups depicted? Why were measurements taken and

> *An art director who can get his own editor sentenced to prison may be said to have achieved the highest goal to which an art director can aspire.*
>
> — *Otto Friedrich*

to whose advantage? First, consider the data collection. Much of the system of polls and academic research works to obscure the reasons behind gathering data. Sometimes the best that editors can do is speculate. What might have motivated the researchers to ask particular questions? Why were the queries phrased in the way they were? Journalists may not have originated the research, but they must take responsibility for publishing it.

Also consider how social groups are depicted. Statistical classifications are inventions. So-called Hispanics, for example, come from dozens of countries and are hardly similar in their customs, foods, or even body types or skin colorations. The category masks considerable antagonism between nationalities as well as diversity among peoples. For insiders, the term *Hispanic* carries racial overtones that emphasize European ancestry and subtly discredit other roots in Africa and pre-Columbian America. For outsiders, the category serves principally to separate and marginalize individuals. Assigning them to a cluster and naming them *Hispanic* makes the grouping seem real (completing a process called *reifying*).

Finally, consider why measurements were taken and who benefits. Most often, the decision to measure certain things assigns relative worth according to a system of values foreign to many individuals in a group. For example, long-term lesbian and gay relationships hardly exist statistically because they are rarely measured. The decision to ignore stable relationships feeds the stereotype that gay men and lesbians can't make commitments. During the 1990 U.S. census, same-sex couples who marked "married" had their forms "corrected," even if they were wed in another country where such unions are legally binding. Most measurements have similar cultural and political implications, favoring some more common or more desirable individuals and groups over others.

Besides evaluating the data, editors need to consider the values inherent in the designs of charts. The standard forms used in newspapers express attitudes toward content and read-

ers. Dark or colorful charts that de-emphasize the text of surrounding stories and large charts that dominate everything on
a page assert a preference for graphic or statistical over textual
content. Whether charts are simple or com-
plex, with a great or small volume of data,
implies a judgment about the competence of
readers. The organization of elements within a
chart may betray an egalitarianism, with many
objects of similar scale and tonal value, or an
exaggerated hierarchy, with objects differenti-
ated visually by layers, ranks, or priority. These
design choices work to exclude some readers,
who may lack the skill to read the charts or
may take the design as a message directed at
some group of a different educational level,
age, or seriousness.

*The press,
like fire, is
an excellent
servant, but
a terrible
master.*

—*James Fenimore
Cooper*

◪ Design decisions spring in part from the
working conditions at newspapers. They may
result from dependence on graphics networks
without the local resources to adjust the content to community needs and tastes. They may result from
reliance on available tools, such as preset computer software.
The background and training of designers and their working
conditions also influence their charts. Editors expect a certain
output from the staff, which can produce many simple, boilerplate charts or fewer original or complex ones that take
longer to design. The aesthetic goals of artists, as Tufte argues,
and their relish for technology sometimes interfere with the
information charts provide. Critical readers may not know
the inner workings of a local newspaper, but the charts themselves do provide some clues about the conditions of design.
Art school–trained designers using networks and computers
often produce highly polished designs that focus on national
statistics.

While they may exclude, belittle, or misrepresent people,
charts can also be used to the opposite effect. Some research

suggests that minority groups may get greater attention and their views more serious consideration as a result of being depicted in graphic form along with mainstream or majority positions (Hollander). When the information is so detailed that individuals can find out about their particular interests and circumstances, then the chart may break down social barriers and historical assumptions about who and what matters. Handling that much information would require inspired design. A few original charts would take as great an investment as the flood of boilerplate now being produced.

Charts and Cultural Values

Besides expressing their own values, editors, in the act of publishing charts, participate in the broader social outlook of the times. Charts are evidence of those cultural values. The literature of political, social, and ideological implications of charts so far is extremely small. Daniel C. Hallin has referred to charts in studies of the media and society at war. A few authors have considered the politics contained in charts (e.g., *Journal*). The view of cognitive and semiotic theorists, that the test of a chart is in the function it performs, leads most researchers to ignore other roles charts play in culture.

Charts probably mark the ascendancy of the values that engender them. The fortunes of chart making seem to rise and decline with commercial and military activity. Charts may also serve as a sort of barometer of technical change. They record the history of statistical assumptions about class, gender, race, and the like. And they contain the residue of the political, economic, and social process of layout and design. Although these values may seem abstract and distant, they do connect with the experiences of newspaper readers.

Statisticians caution that the regularity charts show for large aggregates will not accurately reflect personal experience. Nevertheless, the statistics in charts get applied to individuals in daily practice. Modern societies use charts to build people's physical surroundings, from slums to wealthy enclaves. Charts help determine insurance rates, affect one's chances of getting a business loan or mortgage (and the rate of interest), and may influence representation in government. More important, cultures use charts to create the symbolic environment in which people live. They assign individuals to social classes, categories, and aggregates with a common set of self-fulfilling expectations. These practices converge on the newspaper, where charts solidify the symbolic world. Cautioning readers not to apply the lessons of charts to themselves dodges this practical reality.

Charts also capture the spirit of the times in which individuals live. Although not focused specifically on charts, the histories of numeracy and statistics hint that graphic forms participated in the periodic enthusiasm for numbers. Further study might show that charts increased in popularity during the period of Jacksonian devotion to numeracy, for example. Newspapers have long published more maps during military conflicts, such as the battle plans that illustrated the U.S. Civil War.

> $\mathcal{N}$ewspapers serve as chimneys to carry off noxious vapors and smoke.
>
> — *Thomas Jefferson*

Other forms of charts have flowered during two distinct periods of the twentieth century. The first began in the 1910s and 1920s, when the U.S. military intervened in several countries and sent troops to Europe and when business and wealth expanded in speculative markets. By the 1930s, newspapers in larger cities used charts to cover local as well as foreign events (Figure 3.13), and the *Chicago Tribune* graphics service traces its origins to this first period (Combs). The second began in the 1980s and 1990s, when military interventions and speculative business expansion coincided with the appearance of *USA Today*. The similarities between these two periods have frequently been cited.

FIGURE 3.13.
Hand-drawn
chart from the
early twentieth
century.
*Chicago
Tribune* 1936;
rpt. in
Combs 4.

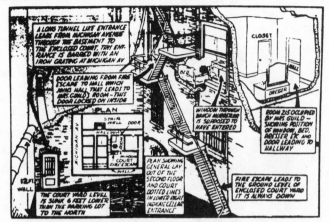

MYSTERIOUSLY SLAIN IN Y. W. C. A. HOTEL

Diagram showing location of the slain Mrs. Lillian Guild's room in Y. W. C. A. hotel and route through courtyard and up fire escape by which slayer may have entered. At the reader's left is a parking lot, on a higher level than the courtyard. From this lot there is a direct view into victim's room.

The increasing use of charts in the twentieth century marked the cultural drift away from the ideal of individualism and toward the concept of the norm in American political and social life (Susman). "We, the people" became "we, the statistical average" as measured in public opinion. Charts often depict aggregates defined by stereotypes that, as Walter Lippmann argued in the 1920s, contribute to the mental images that guide private and political action.

The coverage of war provides a good example. Maps usually show assaults and invasions as clean, smooth arrows, which emphasize directional force while erasing the fear and violence inherent in the events themselves. Diagrams of military apparatus often emphasize their aesthetic power without hinting at the consequences of their use. Tabulations of military conquests assert a policy of equilibrium of forces, casualties, prisoners, or anything else appearing on the list. This sort of war coverage is also evidence of political control, which seeks to make combat sanitary and aesthetic. But it need not be so. Aggregate statistics might just as powerfully show that besides the soldiers killed in fighting, children suffer the greatest casualties of war and, further, that poor children make up the bulk of those.

After the Gulf conflict, my son's chatter continued unabated until we went to see the movie version of *Hamlet*. Besides complaining that the actors "spoke that dialect," my son was dismayed. The intricate web of events in the movie (involving poison, swordplay, and stereotypical pageantry) excited him, matching the complexity of video games, where a multitude of perils accost the player amid the trappings of mythic and clichéd heroism. But then the film action ended, leaving only Horatio to tell the tale. My son's laconic remark, "Everybody died," expressed his bewilderment as well as an empirical observation. The movie had programmed no instant resurrections for a quarter.

Shakespearean tragedy represents human blood and personal strife; information graphics too often do not. The ethical debates about perspective, grids, and decoration, as well as the controversy over vividness and utility, skirt this larger issue. An enthusiasm for publishing charts reveals one of journalism's hidden faces. It is a visage bedecked in the current visual style. Journalists may respond to the urge to follow fashion and use charts because, besides all their other meanings, charts have become a sign of being up-to-date. Whatever the causes of the current enthusiasm, charts will continue to appear in newspapers. Individual charts and the practices that produce them merit careful, critical reading that acknowledges their root meanings from history and their consequences for individuals and society.

CHAPTER 4

JNTERPRETING

TYPOGRAPHY

In Backman Elementary School, where I learned to write,

every classroom was encircled by well-made letters and num-

bers. These formed a border, just above the chalkboards, of

printing in the primary grades and cursive in the intermedi-

ate. The chalkboards were faintly ruled in sets of solid and

broken lines, three for each line of writing. Our report cards

listed grades for penmanship, and my teachers still remembered the days when good handwriting garnered prizes. My own writing, with effort, became legible and neat, although nothing as elaborate as my grandparents'. I could safely ignore my teacher's lecture against writing backhand. And I marveled at the clarity of a left-handed classmate's script, as well as at the contortions the effort required. With all the regimentation, we still managed to put something of our personalities into the seductive drudgery of handwriting. My only vivid memory of one girl is her name: the broad, round *D-e-b-o-r-a-h* extending halfway across her papers, aided by the silent *o* and *h*. The lettering fully embodied her expansive self.

Once I escaped the strictures of elementary school, I flirted with backhand in high school, and in college tried printing with all capital letters, imitating several artists and a businessman I admired. Eventually, I began writing very small and fast on paper with narrow college rules, and I must admit my friends complain about my correspondence and tellers question my signature. So I am hard put to bemoan the fact that my sons, all three of them, have sloppy handwriting. It seems their urges toward personal independence, like my own, come into conflict with the demands of social convention. That struggle is central to all writing and typography: From the earliest manuscripts and books to the twentieth-century typographic movements, people have pushed for expression while society pulled them toward uniformity and clarity.

I do wonder what the general decline of penmanship means. Some educators see it as a symptom of schools that fail to build character. Schools may teach facts, they say, but students don't learn to concentrate on or persevere in detailed tasks. At the age when I was engaged in the labor of penmanship, my sons were struggling to write and draw on a computer. One skill takes as much doggedness as the other. Computer games may make handwriting seem unbearably slow, and word processing may make it seem unnecessary. Is the computer then to blame for bad handwriting? Both ways of writing put some individuals at a disadvantage, although the thick-fingered typist can produce as brilliant or shoddy a prose as can the left-handed writer. Our struggle with technical change illustrates a second theme of typography: that technology does not control but instead reopens debate over the directions innovation should take. Newspapers and other social institutions choose between alternatives that reward some individuals and some ways of thinking but work to the detriment of others.

Successful work on computers requires precision, accuracy, and clarity, as does prize-winning penmanship. One is no easier to achieve than the other. What my sons' sloppy hand and their love of computers have in common is something else: a preference for shortcuts and, above all, speed. These hurried values also hold for computer typography. There are more typefaces built into basic word processors than Benjamin Franklin found in a newspaper print shop. Many are shoddy to the point of cliché, but they're quick to use (Figure 4.1). The technology of Gutenberg was tactile and sensual, the letters set one at a time and pressed into the paper. In place of that craftsmanship and art, computers substitute protocols, defaults, and templates, a sort of design in fast forward. Metal and digital type both illustrate another theme behind typography: that the craft of letterforms expresses the styles of thought and action of the times.

FIGURE 4.1. Computer cliché typefonts. Macintosh bit-mapped fonts.

Geneva

Monaco

Chicago

London

Los Angeles

San Francisco

In a computer environment, the meticulous study of typography — inventing and drawing individual letters with the flattened lead of a grade-school pencil — may seem quixotic, especially for journalists and readers who have no say in a newspaper's typography. But to ignore typographic meanings entirely is to surrender to the agendas of others—usually consultants and researchers whose decisions have profoundly changed the substance as well as the face of journalism.

Exploring the roots that give typography its meaning requires taking a break from high-speed culture. The pause can help prepare readers to observe the subtlety of typographic nuance and editors to make informed typographic choices. The history of letterforms has many parallels in newspapers. Today's publishers look to consultants or scientists where Charlemagne turned to learned clerics, but both periods confront questions of authority, style, and readability. These themes of typographic history take on renewed urgency as the computer, whatever its deleterious effects, promises to put typographic decisions into the hands of more journalists and possibly even readers.

*A*ncient *Letterforms and Power*

To understand typography requires a return to its beginnings in handwriting (Goldberg; Meggs). The mark of one's own hand may be a sign of the self, entirely idiosyncratic and original, but even a signature is socially restrained. It must remain fairly consistent to have meaning to others. Writing is not random but follows a script, which in the original sense denotes the forms of letters followed by the writer. Writing, then, is the act of tracing socially agreed-on forms. But these are not entirely of society's making, any more than they are entirely of one's own. This duality has been reduced to the norm called *penmanship* and elevated to the decorative art of *calligraphy*.

The deepest root of typography reaches back to the individual act of drawing. Each letter of the alphabet can be traced to its origins in prehistoric art (Diringer; Anderson). The most cited example is the capital *A*, which began as a drawing of the head of an ox. In the picture writing of India and elsewhere, drawing and writing were the same act. The way to write *ox* was to draw an ox. The vocabulary of written language denoted concrete objects that could be seen and drawn. But the manner of drawing—the set of details used to depict the ox—became fixed by convention. These drawings slowly simplified into a set of characters sometimes called *pictographs*. In semiotic terms, pictographs can be considered icons, signs that resemble their referents in the physical world.

Social convention limited the modes of depiction but also allowed writing to take on a greater range of meanings. In Sumerian and Egyptian writing, drawings came to stand for ideas. The ox was used in cultivation, and its drawn character, simplified to a vee (for the muzzle and horns) crossed by a horizontal line (for the brow and ears), came to signify *food*. These related meanings—ox, agriculture, food, and so forth—belong to the same paradigm, in semiotic terms. Drawings that refer to ideas continue to be used. Written Chinese, for example, has ten thousand such ideograms (Figure 4.2). Early ideograms were iconic, like pictographs, but their meanings could also be abstract.

The drawn characters that became the Western alphabet began to lose their references to physical objects between 1600 and 1000 B.C.E. A Semitic innovation, disseminated by the Phoenicians of that time, was to use characters to refer to the sounds of language, rather than directly to objects or ideas. These transformed phonetic characters, called *symbols* in semiotics, are arbitrary, unlike earlier characters whose forms were motivated (tied to the mental concepts they signified). The ox character, turned on its ear (like the "less than" symbol in mathematics, crossed with a vertical line), would have taken the initial sound of the word for ox, *aleph*, had the Semites written any vowels. Instead, the symbol became a period or stop. (A better example is the letter *B*, the first sound of the word *beth*, meaning "house.")

In the classical era, technical refinements made the alpha-

FIGURE 4.2. Chinese ideograms. *Top*, Tung (the east), the sun rising behind trees. *Bottom*, Kao (open sky), the sun risen above treetops. From Michael Cardew, "Design and Meaning in Preliterate Art," in Michael Greenhalgh and Vincent Megaw, *Art in Society: Studies in Style, Culture, and Aesthetics* (New York: St. Martin's Press, 1978) 16.

113

FIGURE 4.3.
Brush origin
of the serif.
Left, freely
written letter
by E. M.
Catich. *Right*,
redrawn letter
from the
Trajan
Inscription in
Rome. From
Catich
228–29.

bet a more precise social instrument but continued to reflect the human hand in action. From 900 to 400 B.C.E., the Greeks added vowels and adapted the Semitic names for letters: *alpha*, *beta*, and so forth (Humez and Humez). After 400 B.C.E., the Romans adapted this twenty-character alphabet by altering the forms of eight of the letters (*C, D, G, L, P, R, S,* and *V*) and adding two more (*F* and *Q*). These adjustments reduced the ambiguity of written sounds, thereby increasing control, while the physical practices of writing or inscribing letterforms influenced their shapes. Capital Roman letters, or *majuscules*, originated in drawn forms but reached the summit of their visual evolution in lapidary (the craft of inscribing stone monuments), and their shapes descended from the brush (Figure 4.3) used to plan the inscriptions that were then chiselled and painted in by hand (Catich). Small letters, or *minuscules*, developed slowly from the pen used in handwriting. How people held these tools has continued to influence the design of letterforms.

The end of the Roman Empire saw the flowering of regional autonomy and diversity in letterforms. During the early Middle Ages, scribes developed many distinctive minuscules, as well as cursives and uncials (Anderson; Jackson). Cursives are slanted letters, and uncials are rounded and curved capital letters; the visual character of both forms arises from the angle and motion of the hand and pen during writing. These scripts flourished regionally. In the British Isles, the Irish and Anglo-Saxons developed their own versions. On the Continent, letterforms of the Merovingian dynasty of Gaul and Germany differed from those of the Visigothic monarchy of southern France and Spain. The Italian peninsula had three common designs, centered in the northern Lombardic, central Roman, and southern Beneventan regions.

Greater uniformity and control emerged as political power, wealth, and learning became more centralized. When Charlemagne imposed Frankish rule, extending from Ireland and England to northern Italy and from Spain to the Elbe in Germany, he also imposed on the welter of scripts a common language and form of lettering (Anderson). He attracted scholars from throughout the empire, among them Alcuin of York, who established schools, supervised the copying of manuscripts, and produced a definitive text of the Bible. The scriptorium of Abbot York set the pattern for a double alphabet, called the Carolingian script (Figure 4.4), by combining small letters from his native Northumbrian handwriting with Roman capital letters.

The history of the Western alphabet unfolds as a continual push and pull between local autonomy and central control. Handwriting and drawing allowed a diversity of individual expression, which became disciplined through the social necessity to expand the range of meanings and the degree of abstraction open to written depiction. Changes in techniques also made the alphabet a more precise social tool, while

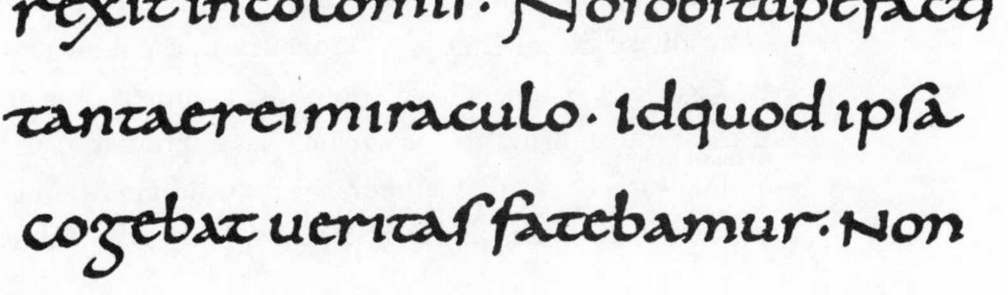

FIGURE 4.4. Carolingian minuscule, early ninth century. Fig. 1 in *On Type Designs Past and Present*, by Stanley Morison (London: Benn, 1962) 16.

encouraging personal experimentation. The tug-of-war between greater uniformity and local diversity paralleled the rise and decline of centralized power in Europe. Although the context differs, the choice of text typography at newspapers gets worked out through a similar set of forces: The autonomy of editors is limited by the conventions of journalism and the economic and political power of owners and publishers, who rely on expert consultants. Technical change does not necessarily favor one side over the other.

Stylistic Change and the Manuscript Tradition

Throughout history, stylistic change has marked the shifting boundary between these competing claims, which combine in what Heinrich Wolfflin's classic study calls the dual root of style. Manuscripts created before the advent of printing provide an early record of the patterns of style in letterforms (Chappell). Scribes produced manuscripts that adapted and changed, as well as copied and reproduced, what had gone before. Their work took on resemblances to the local school of lettering as well as style similarities within a developing national or regional tradition. Schools and styles of letterforms embody the complex cultural, practical, and temporal pattern of stylistic change.

Style is a cultural distillation of what in German is called *Zeitgeist*, the spirit or general trend of thought and feeling. In Europe, the decentralization common early in the Middle Ages returned with the dissolution of the Carolingian house and the weakness of subsequent secular empires, but the Roman church gradually rose to be the center of economic and military life in Europe, a tendency that culminated with the Crusades. Scholars have noted that an upreaching attitude of the time, aspiring to the divine, was expressed in religious architecture (Nolan). Cathedrals of the High Middle Ages had soaring pillars, flying buttresses, and spiky gables and

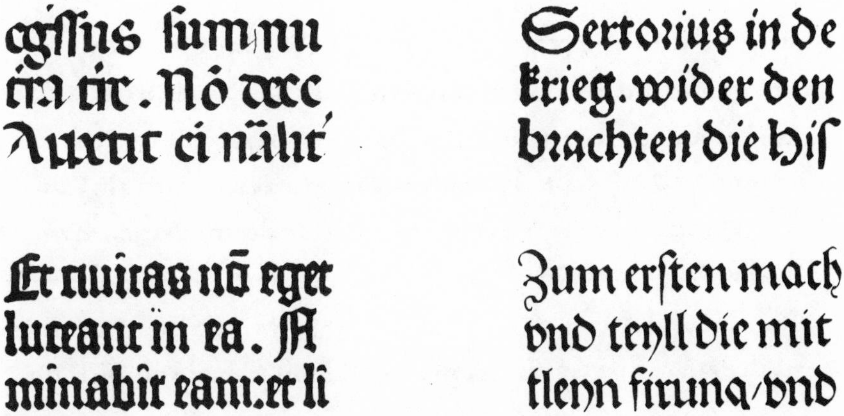

cgffus fummu
tra tir. Nõ ccc
Auxtir ci nälir

Sertonius in de
krieg. wider den
brachten die hif

Et muitas nõ eget
luteaunt in ea. fA
minabir eanuer li

Zum erften mach
vnd teyll die mit
flenn firung/vnd

FIGURE 4.5. Gothic schools. *Top left*, Rotunda, thirteenth century. *Bottom left*, Textura, fourteenth and fifteenth centuries. *Top right*, Schwabacher, sixteenth century. *Bottom right*, Fraktur, sixteenth and seventeenth centuries. From Ruegg and Frolich 214–15.

crockets, contrasting with the fine tracery of foils and stained-glass window frames. This style, which later acquired the name *Gothic*, appeared in many other arts, from painting to crafts.

In letterforms, *black-letter* style illustrates the role of stylistic change. In the twelfth century, the Carolingian script evolved into several forms of writing that were dark, more compressed and vertical, and more tightly spaced together, with angular terminals. The capital letters were embellished with fine lines crossing or echoing the heavy strokes. These black and spiky letters embodied in calligraphy the Gothic style of architecture (Ruegg and Frohlich). The scribes copying manuscripts worked within a local tradition, and their individual variations belonged to the same school of letterforms. Several schools emerged, such as the rounded Rotunda of northern Italy and the Textura of the Netherlands (see Figure 4.5). These black-letter schools were eventually replaced by a resurgence of Carolingian-inspired letterforms, beginning in Italy with what became known as the *humanistic hand* (Figure 4.6). These two early styles had variations (the humanistic had fewer because it was consciously modeled after earlier manuscripts) that coexisted, coming in and out of fashion in particular locales.

From the example of manuscript letterforms, several obser-

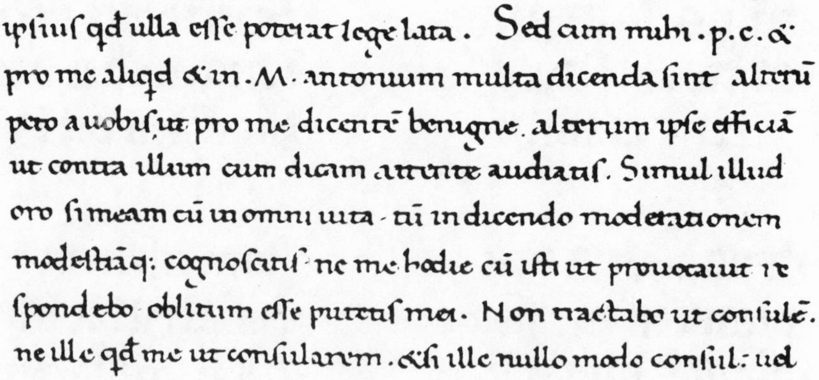

ipſiuſqd ulla eſſe poteiat leqe lata . Sed cum mihi .p.c. &
pro me aliqd & in .M. antonium multa dicenda ſint alterū
peto a uobiſ ut pro me dicente benigne. alterum ipſe efficia
ut contra illum cum dicam attente audiatiſ. Simul illud
oro ſi meam cū in omni uita · tū in dicendo moderationem
modeſtiaq: coqnoſcatiſ ne me hodie cū iſti ut prouocauit it
ſpondebo oblitum eſſe putetiſ mei. Non tactabo ut conſule.
ne ille qd me ut conſularem . &ſi ille nullo modo conſuli: uel

FIGURE 4.6.
Humanistic
hand. Written
by Poggio, c.
1425, Cicero,
Phil. II. 10
(Florence,
Laur. 48, 22, f.
9r). Pl. XV in
*Ancient Writing
and Its
Influence,* by
B. L. Ullman
(New York:
Longmans,
1932).

vations can be made about the history of stylistic change. Black letter emerged slowly from existing scripts and, rather than completely supplanting them, evolved with them. The style was not unitary but a pattern found in many samples and schools tied to particular places in time. These observations suggest several generalizations about stylistic change. As fashions in art and decoration evolve, new letter designs also appear, reflecting and contributing to the style of the time. New styles rarely spring up suddenly but instead emerge gradually, metamorphosing from previous styles. They do not simply prevail for a period and then change but instead work themselves out in relation to other styles.

Style is also a product of historical and ethical thinking. Only in history does the process fall at all neatly into periods. Practitioners and scholars search for the visual patterns in what has gone before, and their descriptions and nomenclature are not purely historical but also play against or with contemporary work. *Gothic,* for example, originated as a pejorative term (Deuchler) used to condemn the style in favor of what was considered a classical ideal. Discussions of style often turn on moral judgments, pitting concepts of the good and beautiful against the bad, spent, or ugly. Newspapers change stylistically as industry standards compete with the demand of journalists and readers for a particular and local product. Newspaper typography participates in the prevailing *Zeitgeist*, and so old clippings or pages seem redolent of their era.

Typography and Technical Change after Gutenberg

The development of movable type, ascribed to Johannes Gutenberg in the mid-1400s, is thought to have hardened the letterforms not only physically but also culturally. The impact of print culture on the early modern era has been explored by Elizabeth Eisenstein and others (e.g., Chartier), in part in response to Harold Innis and Marshall McLuhan. In place of the gradualism of manuscript practices, typography substituted metal letters that imitated calligraphy and made changes cumbersome and costly. But the scribes and copyists had not been entirely free to invent and follow fashion. The scriptoria where they worked imposed controls to produce a fairly consistent output. Nor did mechanical printing always result in uniformity. The typographers of the incunabula, the earliest books produced with movable type, often made changes midstream.

In other words, the separation of typography from calligraphy is often overstated. Gutenberg and his fellow goldsmiths in Mainz, Germany, came along not at the birth but, instead, well into the middle of a larger history full of technical changes (Warner). In the history of letterforms, changing techniques substituted new rigidities for old but also opened new avenues for varied exploration. Typographic technology changed practices and vocabulary, but the central patterns of the history of letterforms continued after Gutenberg: a permanence or uniformity (*synchrony*, in semiotic terms) as typographers repeatedly imitated and revived forms within the constant framework of the alphabet, and a dynamism or variety (*diachrony*) as typographers adapted and altered the forms, often in conflict with one another.

Synchrony can be found in the consistency of the alphabet. Letters have been added only rarely, three of them (*j*, *u*, and *w*) since Gutenberg. European languages eventually added diacritical markings (such as the cedilla [,] and tilde [~]) to draw distinctions between similar sounds. Likewise, punctuation marks, which had emerged in manuscripts, became widespread, although employed slightly differently in each language. But the letters themselves have remained stable. The dual alphabets, minuscule and majuscule, have also remained constant. Bauhaus designers and legibility researchers, who sought in the twentieth century to eliminate this duality (which they considered inefficient), met with little success. The Western alphabet has proved resistant to change, providing a secure framework for particular and stylistic variations.

Diachrony can be found in two patterns of typographic variation, one cyclical, unpredictable, or reversible, the other more permanent and unidirectional. Particular changes by typefounders (and their heirs, the computer type designers) can lead to either pattern. Some, such as the humanistic types of Simon de Colines (Amert), continue in use and exert influence for centuries. Others appear and flourish for a time, later to be ignored and lost or perhaps to reappear. Both patterns of change produce many typefaces that resemble one another. The term *school* can refer both to the many derivations from a single design, such as the Colines-inspired types that constitute the Garamond group, and also to a range of individual type designs that share certain physical and historical features (to be described later in this chapter).

Although individual types have an uncertain fate, the diachrony of style is unidirectional. Types and schools may come and go, but the style they share remains a permanent part of the typographic repertoire, even though its range of uses may change. For example, the style of *italics* descends from several designs, including one by Francesco Griffo for

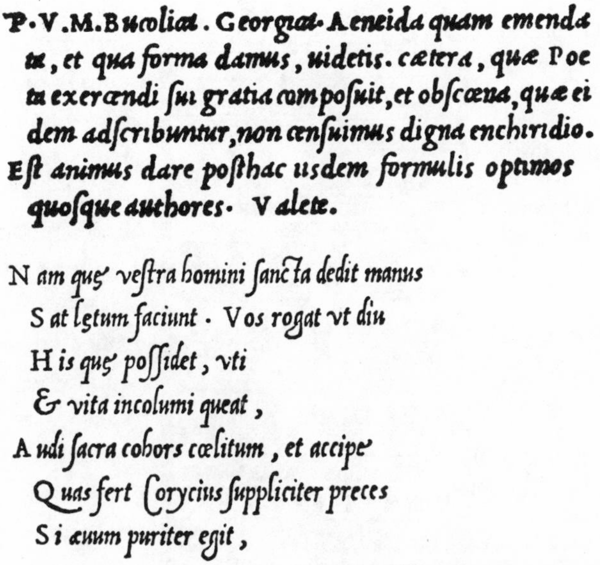

FIGURE 4.7
Italic typogra-
phy. *Top*, Aldus
Manutius,
Venice, 1501.
From Morison
and Jackson
57. *Bottom*,
Ludovico degli
Arrighi,
Rome, 1524.
Fig. 23 in *On
Type Designs
Past and
Present*, by
Stanley
Morison
(London:
Benn, 1962) 36.

P·V·M.Bucolica. Georgica· Aeneida quam emenda
ta, et qua forma damus, uidetis. caetera, quae Poe
ta exercendi sui gratia compofuit, et obfcoena, quae ei
dem adfcribuntur, non cenfuimus digna enchiridio.
Eft animus dare pofthac usdem formulis optimos
quofque authores· Valete.

N am que veftra homini fanc̄la dedit manus
S at lętum faciunt · Vos rogat vt diu
H is que poffidet, vti
& vita incolumi queat,
A udi facra cohors coelitum, et accipe
Q uas fert Corycius fuppliciter preces
S i auum puriter egit,

the printer-publisher Aldus Manutius in the late fifteenth
century (Updike) (Figure 4.7). Italics were at first used to set
entire books economically for a growing commerce. The letters fit snugly together like the slanted, often connected forms
of cursive handwriting. Although many faces and schools of
italics stand alone, in running text the style is now commonly
used to provide typographic emphasis.

Besides italics, two other styles with ties to scribes and to
early typographers are also ancillary. *Decorative type* emerged
from the initial letters of illuminated manuscripts and has flourished principally in advertising display since the nineteenth
century (Figure 4.8). It now appears in a range of novelties
fashioned after everything from Broadway lights and hairpins
to op art. *Imitative type*, inspired by older calligraphic scripts,
also includes recent forms such as typewriter and stencil lettering. These styles are not firmly delineated, and several systems of
typographic classification compete for acceptance (Lawson,
Printing; Perfect and Rookledge). Most systems classify type by
the formal appearance of its letters or by reference to the historical roots of style.

FIGURE 4.8.
Decorative
advertising
typography.
Circus hand-
bill, c. 1840.
Rpt. in
Lawson
Printing 32.

The diachrony of conflict and change as well as the synchrony of imitation and revival are best illustrated by the interplay of Gothic and humanistic styles after Gutenberg. Early typographers made letters that imitated the Gothic style then in vogue. They reflected local variations and contrasting formal and private uses. The many individual variants originating in printed books of fifteenth- and sixteenth-century Europe add up to several schools of black-letter type. Schwabacher, Fraktur, and Kurrent (besides Textura and Rotunda, mentioned with their origins in manuscript lettering; see Figure 4.5, p. 117) in turn add up to the black-letter style. Historians of printing have traced the early conflicts between the Gothic black-letter and humanistic roman typography, identifying the printers and books that brought *roman* typefaces into the ascendant in each European country (H. Carter). The roman faces were imitated in turn, but black-letter typography persisted in Germany and Scandinavia for centuries and continues to be revived today.

These diachronic and synchronic patterns (White) have recurred throughout typographic history. The nineteenth century saw many innovations in advertising display and Art Nouveau typefaces, as well as the homage to late medieval forms by William Morris and the Arts and Crafts movement. In the twentieth century, Bauhaus and the New Typography forwarded an efficient and functional modernism in reaction to what were considered the decorative excesses of the previous century. Modern asymmetry in turn was challenged by what has become known as the classic typographic style, inspired by Morris to resurrect (but also adapt) older forms. The styles of each succeeding age have permanently expanded the wardrobe of the Western alphabet. Many costumes suited a passing fancy and then were lost, but the framework of letters, however dressed, has endured.

In the editorial side of newspaper typography, roman typefaces dominate, decorative and imitative letters are rare in the news columns, and many papers use quotation marks to avoid the inconvenience of setting italics in body type. Some earlier typographic conflicts have reached a truce in newspapers. Black-letter nameplates coexist with roman body type, and plain, bold display types from nineteenth-century advertising, once disparaged with the derogatory name *grotesques*, now serve as headline faces. Although not the focus of this chapter, advertising typography follows its own intents and conventions, which have directly influenced editorial typography. As new typographic styles appear, often on newspaper pages in the advertising side, they are usually met with strong resistance by the news side, only to be assimilated and widely imitated (see Chapter 5). These changes are most often attributed to technology, in an oversimplification akin to beliefs about Gutenberg.

*H*istorical Schools of Roman Type

Because it dominates not only newspapers but all print media, roman type deserves particular attention. Typographers usually divide the style into several schools. The largest school, *old style*, has three principal subgroups (Figure 4.9). The oldest is

FIGURE 4.9.
Old style
school. *Top,*
Nicolas
Jenson,
Venice, 1470,
Eusebius, *De
Preparatione
Evangelica*
(reduced).
Center, roman
type attributed
to Claude
Garamond,
used by
Charles
Estienne,
Paris, 1549
(reduced).
Bottom,
William
Caslon,
specimen
broadside,
London,
1734
(reduced).
Figs. 27, 169,
and 262 in
Updike.

qui omnibus ui aquarum fubmerfis cum filiis fuis fimul ac nuribus mirabili quodã modo quafi femen huãni generis conferuatus eft:quẽ utinã quafi uiuam quandam imaginem imitari nobis contingat:& hi quidem ante diluuium fuerunt:poft diluuium autem alii quorũ unus altiffimi dei facerdos iuftitiæ ac pietatis miraculo rex iuftus lingua he- bræorũ appellatus eft:apud quos nec circuncifionis nec mofaicæ legis ulla mentio erat. Quare nec iudæos(pofteris eni hoc nomen fuit)neq; gentiles:quoniam non ut gentes pluralitatem deorum inducebant fed hebræos proprie noïamus aut ab Hebere ut dictũ eft:aut qã id nomen

ETVS TATEM nobi- liffimæ Vicecomitum fami- liæ qui ambitiofius à præalta Romanorũ Cæfarum origi- ne, Longobardífq; regibus deducto ftemmate, repete- re contẽdunt, fabulofis pe- nè initiis inuoluere viden- tur. Nos autem recentiora illuftrioráque,vti ab omnibus recepta,fequemur:cõ- tentique erimus infigni memoria Heriprandi & Gal-

By W. CASLON, Letter-Founder

ABCD
ABCDE

DOUBLE PICA ROMAN.
Quoufque tandem abutere, Cati- lina, patientia noftra? quamdiu nos etiam furor ifte tuus eludet? quem ad finem fefe effrenata jac- ABCDEFGHJIKLMNOP

based on the humanistic hand imitated by printers in Italy before 1500. *Venetian old style,* as it is called, has low con- trast between thick and thin in the strokes and was consid- ered ideal for publishing classical texts during the Re- naissance. Recent Venetian typefaces descend from the designs of Nicolas Jenson, a Frenchman who learned printing in Germany and then settled in Venice just before 1470.

Imitations of his designs usually reproduce the effects of humanistic calligraphy. The angle of the broad pen used by calligraphers produced a tilted crossbar in the lowercase *e*, a left-leaning slant in the axis of the curves (best seen in the interior white spaces or *counters*), and another diagonal in some of the terminals, or *serifs*, of the ascending strokes.

Subsequent letterforms slowly lost the calligraphic features found in Venetian type (H. Carter). The *French old styles* retained the diagonal stress of the counters and the inclined upper serifs but altered the relation between thick and thin strokes and leveled the crossbar of the *e*. The most imitated of the French old styles is the design named for Claude Garamond, who cut and cast type in Paris in the mid–sixteenth century. Late in the century, the center of typographic design moved to the Low Countries and from there to England in the seventeenth century. *Dutch-English old styles* further increased the contrast in the strokes and left even fewer diagonal stresses. The designs generally imitate the work by Anton Janson in Holland and by William Caslon of England.

The second school of roman typefaces, the *transitional*, accompanied the beginning of the Enlightenment (Figure 4.10). Many transitional romans descend from the designs of John Baskerville, who worked in Birmingham, England, in the mid–eighteenth century. *Transitional* refers to the period when the last of the calligraphic effects disappeared from typography. In the early transitionals, such as the designs by Baskerville, the stresses in the letters tilt only slightly to the left or not at all, and the contrast between thin and thick strokes is increased. Later versions, such as Cheltenham, flatten the slanted ascending serifs and reduce the overall contrast. Most body typography in newspapers has structural features similar to those of this later form of the transitional romans.

In the place of the intuitive basis of calligraphy, transitional designs began to introduce a rational basis for the construction of letters. The antecedents for this philosophical change

FIGURE 4.10.
Transition
from the old
style. *Top*,
Philippe
Grandjean de
Fouchy,
Romain du roi,
1702
(reduced).
Rpt. in Allen
Hutt, *Fournier:
The Compleat
Typographer*
(Totowa:
Rowman,
1972) 8.
Center, Pierre-
Simon
Fournier (le
jeune), *Modèles
des Caractères*,
Paris, 1742
(enlarged). Fig.
181 in
Updike, vol.
1. *Bottom*,
John
Baskerville,
Birmingham,
1761
(reduced). Fig.
40 in Morison
On Type 53.

La première époque vous présente d'abord un grand spectacle : Dieu qui crée le ciel et la terre par sa parole, et qui fait l'homme à son image. C'est par où commence Moïse, le plus ancien

ON revêtit les uns de peaux de bêtes ſauvages, & enſuite on lâcha contre eux des chiens affamez ; on en expoſa d'autres aux lions dans l'amphi-théatre ; & on attacha les autres à des poteaux, ou ils furent tous brulez vifs.

TANDEM aliquando, Quiri-tes! L. Catilinam furentem audacia, ſcelus anhelantem, pe-ABCDEFGHIJKLMN.

began when the French Academy prepared letterforms on a grid following mathematical proportions, after Louis XIV commissioned a new type design at the beginning of the eighteenth century. This *romain du roi* alphabet inspired many French imitators, notably Pierre-Simon Fournier and several generations of the Didot family, whose designs bridge the divide between the transitional and the next roman classifica-tion, modern.

With the *modern school*, the design of roman type rigorous-ly substituted the rational ideal for any remaining calligraphic

FIGURE 4.11.
Modern
school. *Top*,
Giambattista
Bodoni,
Parma, c.
1780. Fig. 42
in Morison *On
Type* 57.
Center,
William
Martin,
"Baydell
Shakespeare"
for Bulmer,
London, 1792
(reduced). Fig.
297 in Updike,
vol. 2.
Bottom, Pierre
Didot, folio
Horace, 1799
(reduced). Fig.
167 in Updike,
vol. 1.

ottimamente fatte. Che però la gra-
zia della scrittura forse più che in al-
tro sta in certa disinvoltura di tratti
franchi, risoluti, spediti, e nondime-
no così nelle forme esatti, così degra-
dati ne' pieni, *che non trova l'invidia
ove gli emende.* Ma forse più sicuro

Enter Julia, and Lucetta.

Jul. But say, Lucetta, now we are alone,
Would'st thou then counsel me to fall in love?
Luc. Ay, madam; so you stumble not unheedfully.
Jul. Of all the fair resort of gentlemen,
That every day with parle encounter me,
In thy opinion, which is worthiest love?
Luc. Please you, repeat their names, I'll show my mind

ODE I.

AD VENEREM.

Intermissa, Venus, diu
Rursus bella moves. Parce, precor, precor!
Non sum qualis eram bonæ
Sub regno Cinaræ. Desine, dulcium
Mater sæva Cupidinum,
Circa lustra decem flectere mollibus

127

influences. A highly rationalist design for letters, very much in tune with the elegant and refined tastes of the time, was accomplished by Giambattista Bodoni, who apprenticed at the Vatican Press and then worked for the dukes of Parma. In modern typefaces such as Didot and Bodoni, the contrast between thick and thin strokes has become abrupt, the serifs have lost any slant, and the curved brackets that joined serifs to the main strokes have all but vanished (Figure 4.11). Modern designs, tied to France as a center of fashion in advertising, have been repeatedly imitated in newspaper headline typography.

In reaction to the Industrial Revolution, movements in art and decoration turned away from the rational ideal. The nostalgia of the nineteenth century inspired a classical revival and a fascination with exotic civilizations. The fourth school of roman type, called *square serif*, imitated the angles and postures found in hieroglyphics by thickening the serifs, hence its description as *slab serif* or *Egyptian* (Figure 4.12). One subgroup of Egyptians retains the slight thicks and thins of the later transitional faces, along with a vestigial bracket. The best-known faces of this subgroup are the Clarendons, introduced in 1845 by Robert Beasley and used widely in newspaper headlines of the mid–twentieth century. The larger, more important subgroup of the square-serif school, with serifs as thick as the strokes (or nearly so), is best known through the imitators of Stymie, designed by Morris F. Benton in 1931.

The final school of the roman style, *sans serif*, is shorn of the last vestige of the brush and chisel. Typefounders introduced the sans-serif school in the nineteenth century under a variety of names, including *grotesque*, *Gothic*, and *Egyptian* (the latter two adding a confusing duplication). The earliest sans serifs were used in advertising display in 1816, but the style gained wide acceptance only recently (Figure 4.13). The severe and unadorned letters were adopted by the artistic avant-garde in the 1920s. Futura, a design Paul Renner introduced in 1927, was widely imitated in newspaper headlines of the 1950s. The typographic innovations of Herbert Bayer and the Bauhaus did not achieve wide commercial acceptance at first, although the efforts of Jan Tschichold did give the New Typography some commercial success early on in Germany. Widespread acceptance came much later, with the introduction in 1957 of Univers, designed by Adrian Frutiger. At about that time, Max Miedinger's Helvetica appeared and set off the myriad imitations and permutations, leading two decades later to its dominance as a newspaper headline typeface.

These five schools of roman type dominate newspaper typography today (Lawson, *Anatomy*). Body type ranges from old style through modern, with most newspapers using faces of a late transitional design. Headlines vary widely, but a newspaper may select one or combine several old styles, tran-

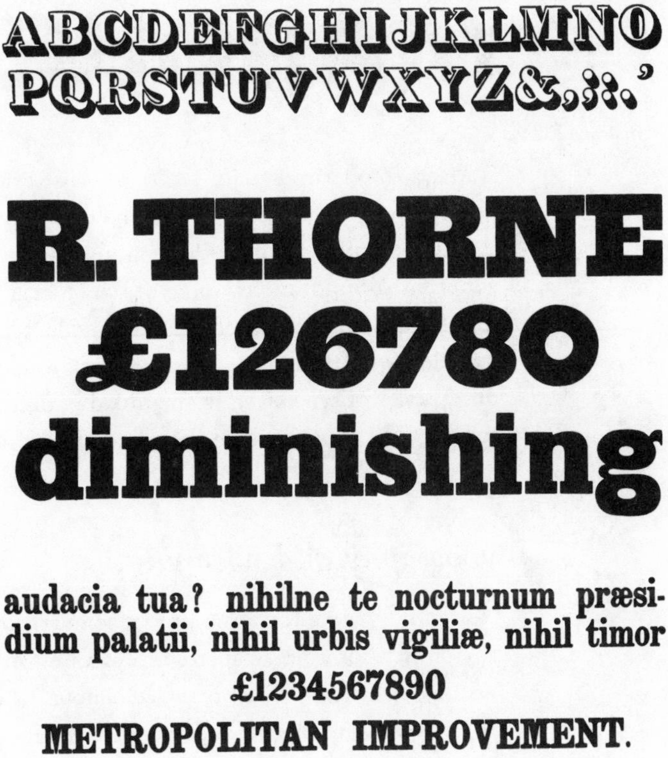

FIGURE 4.12. Egyptian school. *Top*, Vincent Figgins foundry, London, Two-Lines Pica Antique, 1817 (reduced). *Center*, William Thorowgood foundry, London, Six-Lines Pica Egyptian, 1821 (reduced). *Bottom*, William Thorowgood foundry, London, Two-Lines English Clarendon, 1848 (reduced). From Lawson *Anatomy* 310, 312.

FIGURE 4.13.
Sans-serif
school. *Top*,
William
Caslon IV,
London, c.
1816. Fig. 57
in Morison *On
Type* 62.
Center,
Schelter and
Giesecke
foundry,
Germany, c.
1825
(enlarged).
From Lawson
Anatomy 297.
Bottom,
George Bruce,
United States,
c. 1853
(enlarged).
From Lawson
Anatomy 297.

W CASLON JUNR LETTERFOUNDER

venezianischer Porträtmalerei

MARCHES

sitionals, moderns, square serifs, or sans serifs. The editorial side of newspapers in the twentieth century has lagged behind the typographic avant-garde, waiting about twenty years to adopt visual innovations, some of which originate in advertising. By the time they reach the news side, typefaces are heavily laden with meanings. The history of roman schools and of other styles of type, even in the broad outlines described here, can provide some clues for decoding what typography means.

Typography and Meaning

Practitioners have for some time recognized that the typography chosen for a newspaper conveys a host of meanings (e.g., Whitehill; Harum). Each typeface denotes its origins in history as well as the objects and the settings for which it is commonly employed. These customary ties invoke many connotations—the ideas a society comes to associate with certain places and things. Although readers do not usually know typographic history, they still may grasp typographic connotations because they are exposed daily to type that reiterates historical ties and traditional ideas. Studies of typographic connotation (to be described later in this chapter) reveal a general agreement between professional and lay interpretations.

The denotations of the black-letter style are all too obvious. Black letter is a sign of the Gutenberg Bible and other early printed books. Black-letter printing joins with cathedrals and other artifacts of the period as signs of the Gothic style (Figure 4.14). The use of black letter also denotes church inscriptions and titles, especially in the Anglican tradition. Another denotation is found in the signs of antique dealers. These English and antique meanings fuse in the name *Old English*, a term used to label specific typefaces and often employed at newspapers to identify the entire style. Black letter also appears commonly in the signs of pastry shops and other purveyors of hand- or homemade goods. Denoting its common use in the Germanic states, black letter has become

FIGURE 4.14. Gothic book pages. "Crucifixion and Adoration of the Magi," Jean Pucelle, *Petites Heures of Jeanne D'Evreaux* (1325-28, Cloisters Collection, Metropolitan Museum of Art [54.1.2]).Pl. 191 in Deuchler.

a typographic cliché for anything German, on par with leder-hosen, beer steins, and Oktoberfest. And, of course, the style is ubiquitous in newspaper nameplates.

The ideas associated with these customary uses and settings make up the connotations of black letter. Its history as a holdover from manuscripts supplies a backward-looking con-servatism. Black letter also connotes a mysticism involving reli-gion and nature, as symbolized by the woods of Germany, which tower like Gothic forms in the modern imagination. Its link with these forms adds all the romantic connotations of the nineteenth-century Gothic revival that turned away from the Industrial Age, yearning instead for things ancient and myste-rious. These connotations might be summarized in the ideas of religious faith, antiquity, quaintness, handicraft, and conser-vatism, especially when tied to all things German and English.

A black-letter newspaper nameplate might be interpreted to suggest that the bearer is authoritative and traditional, per-haps with a spiritual or visionary mission rooted in or honor-ing nineteenth-century values. Whether that nameplate is appropriate depends on an ethical judgment. Whom does the newspaper serve? Claims to authority and tradition may prop up the industry and fulfill the professional aspirations of jour-nalists. Ties to Victorian values may attract and sustain some readers but not others.

This interpretation ignores the nuances of meaning that particular faces and schools of black-letter type convey. The *New York Times*, for instance, uses narrow letters akin to the bold and impenetrable Textura, drawn with a mechanical pre-cision that makes the nameplate even more forbidding. In contrast, many local newspapers use a broad, open black let-ter, closer to the spirit of Rotunda, which may connote more of a sense of accessibility. A glance at the nameplates on any large newsstand will reveal how diverse even a style as mar-ginalized as black letter can be. Selecting a typeface requires research into history and contemporary practice, as well as a thorough study of the newspaper and its readers.

Generalizations about roman typefaces, even more than the less common styles, are fraught with complexities. The history and use of each school comes laden with libertarian, commercial, aesthetic, and political values. For example, headlines of the modern school convey the rationalist ideal of the Enlightenment, along with a refinement that is aristocratic in orientation. Sans-serif headlines invoke nineteenth-century commercial values even as they espouse an unembellished modernism. These school connotations only begin to reveal typographic meanings.

The forms of roman typefaces also resonate with significance from the general history of letterforms. All sans serifs, for example, are not interchangeable but have formal antecedents among other roman schools and other styles as well. Futura capitals share the broad proportions of humanistic calligraphy and of old-style typography, whereas Helvetica capitals have narrower dimensions, more akin to the black-letter style and to the modern school. A faint echo of the conflicts between humanistic and Gothic forms accompanied the shift from the Futura headlines of the 1940s and 1950s to Helvetica in the 1970s and 1980s. The form of each of these typefaces harks back to forebears that are not merely historical or distant but continue in contemporary use.

The cultural and social values that predominate in any period when a typeface is heavily used also contribute to its meaning. Cheltenham, a late transitional face that verges on square serif, had two heydays as a twentieth-century headline typeface (Figure 4.15). The first occurred during the 1910s and 1920s, a period marked by continuing recession in agriculture, an increasingly dormant labor movement, the speculative boom, strong corporate dominance, and the rise of new electricity-based industries. When these conditions changed and attitudes toward them soured in the 1930s, the typeface associated with the era fell into disuse. Cheltenham languished for sixty years, until similar circumstances welcomed its return to some newspapers at the end of the twentieth century.

FIGURE 4.15.
Cheltenham
newspaper
headlines.
Specimen
page,
*Newspaper
Headings: The
Linotype Way*
(New York:
Merganthaler
Linotype,
1919) 49.

TO ENLIST THE HOUSEWIVES IN CAMPAIGN TO CONSERVE FOOD

Women to Be Instructed So That We Can Eat Wisely and Without Waste—Vegetables to Be Used to Save Staples More Easily Kept.

Washington, May 27.—Enlistment of the country's housewives into the services of the food administrator to accomplish conservation in the home is one of the first tasks to be undertaken by Herbert C. Hoover as food administrator. The women will be recruited, Mr. Hoover announced today, through the aid of state food councils, state officials, the Woman's National Defence Council and civic associations.

"It is the idea of the food administration," said Mr. Hoover today, "to ask every woman who presides over a household to come in as an actual member of the food administration, to be thus entitled to the badges of the administration and to sign a written pledge to carry out the advice and instruction of the food administration as far as her circumstances permit.

New Thrift Propaganda

"It is proposed to divide this vast army into states and direct its activities through the state organizations and state officials. Advice and instruction of a national character will be added to those of the state and local organizations.

"Valuable instruction will in this way be handed down to the individual members from time to time. It is proposed that such advice and instruction should be direct and absolutely specific and to be embraced in the following general lines, all based on the fact that we can eat plenty if we will eat wisely and without waste:

"Elimination of Waste.—Out of our abundance have grown many careless customs that must be curbed. We must learn to imitate the race thrift of the housewife of France, who has so ably sive series of studies of food values and of advantageous buying and preparation of food is to be placed before our women by the agencies now available. Stimulation of the preservation of perishable foods for subsequent use in the household will be encouraged in every way.

"It may well be that the women of America will play a deciding part in the great war if the legislation now pending in regard to the food administration becomes a law."

Russian Committee Will Discuss Terms of Peace

London, May 27.—M. Skobeleff, a member of the executive committee of the Council of Workmen's and Soldiers' Delegates, according to a Reuter dispatch from Petrograd, asserted in his speech Saturday that while the committee of which he is a member was opposed to a separate peace, it is be-

250 Americans Leave Holland on Noordam

First Ship Out Since January Carries 343 Women and Children.

Rotterdam, via London, May 27.—The Holland America Line steamer Noordam sailed for the United States at noon today, having on board a number of Americans. The vessel will proceed through the so-called German "safety zone."

The number of Americans on board is about 250. It includes some fifty sailors who have long been stranded here. There are also a number of Germans and Austrians aboard. Of the 217 persons on the first class list 92 are women or children. There are 251 women or children among the 356 on the second class list. The sailing of the Noordam was delayed by instructions from Germany to discharge beet seed.

Senate and House Conferees Will Take Up Roosevelt Provision Today

Considered Certain That the Measure Will Be Laid Before President.

House and Senate conferees, each bearing instructions from their respective branches of Congress to write into the selective draft army bill the so-called Roosevelt division amendment, will meet tomorrow morning and are expected to act quickly on the subject. Owing to the fact, however, that the action of the House in sending the bill back to conference opens again all the

Disbrow Back in Big Racing Game

Dirt Track Champion to Get Bride's Consent to Again Defend His Title.

Louis Disbrow, king of the dirt track drivers, is to re-enter the racing game. This announcement comes, incidentally, after Disbrow had made public that he was through with the sport, chiefly in deference to a vow he made to his bride, at her request, when she consented to be Mrs. Disbrow.

Disbrow has succeeded in getting his wife to reverse herself on the proposition, and he will appear in various parts of the country for about 10 weeks next summer or in the fall.

every one here and, from telegrams and letters received, thousands in the country are wondering what he will do about yielding to Roosevelt's request to lead to France one of the divisions authorized under the bill.

Frank Mann, Boxer, Is Declared a "Pro"

Frank H. Mann, a boxer, of the Union Settlement Athletic Club, was declared a professional and his registration card

Newspaper body typography derives meaning from a similar pattern of school ties, style resemblances, and period values. Newspapers for the last century have generally rejected the equanimity of early humanistic old styles. For reasons to be presented in detail later in this chapter, newspaper publishers and consultants have favored heavier transitional or Egyptian-inspired faces (Lawson, *Anatomy*). These do homage to the nineteenth-century roots of newspaper practices and also reflect the foreign and exotic emphasis of news.

A distinguishing trait of the newspaper during much of its history has been the intermingling of many typographic styles and schools. The contents of newspapers sport black-letter nameplates, decorative or cursive scripts for the standing titles or "sigs" of columns and regular features, transitional body text, and a selection from the whole array of roman types for headlines. The mixed typography parallels the jumble of content on newspaper pages. Advertising introduces even more typographic diversity, derailing the recent efforts (described in Chapter 5) to clean up the newspaper. Mixed type denotes the nineteenth-century origins and commercial quality of the mass-circulation newspaper and may signal at least broadly an intention (or perhaps a pretension) to address a whole diversity of readers.

Inventing a Twenty-Seventh Letter

*T*ypographic styles and schools are more than abstract historical classifications. They spring from drawing and writing — the way a pen, brush, or chisel is held — and they can be understood best by making examples by hand. Trying to draw different styles of type yourself would be no more than tracing, if you used one of the existing letters. So your first task will be to invent an entirely new letter. Next, you will create many versions of your letter in the forms of the various styles and schools of type. You can then study how your letter would fit with other letters and how it might need to change at different sizes.

Chisels and brushes won't be necessary for this exercise, but you may equip yourself as elaborately as your means allow. A set of calligraphic pens and ink and a set of drawing instruments with a square and compass are probably more than you need. Markers with flat calligraphic tips are less expensive. At a minimum, find a marker with a standard, broad-angled tip, or buy a carpenter's pencil and sharpen the lead to a flat edge. You will also need several sheets of paper, two of them lined, and a fine-tip pen or sharp pencil. With the fine tip, darken every third line on the lined paper to indicate a baseline for each line of lettering. The line above the baseline will mark the x-height, where the small letters normally reach. The spaces above the x-height and below the baseline allow room for the ascenders and descenders. Your lettering will be larger than the size you learned to write in the primary grades, to allow for typographic details.

Use the blank pages to invent a twenty-seventh letter. You may

FIGURE 4.16.
Script typeface
designs. *Top*,
Tamil. *Bottom*,
Devanagari.
Adrian
Frutiger, *Type
Sign Symbol*
(Zurich: ABC
Verlag, 1981)
94, 97.

हिंदी भाषा की पसार-वृद्धि करना उसका विकास
करना ताकि वह भारत की सामाजिक संस्कृति के सब
तत्वों की अभिव्यक्ति का माध्यम हो सके
तथा उसकी आत्मीयता में हस्तक्षेप किए बिना

துபஸிலில் குறிப்பிட்ட மற்றைய இந்திய
துபஸிலில் குறிப்பிட்ட மற்றைய இந்திய

want to refer to languages unfamiliar to you (Figure 4.16). A good place to start is with an inventory of visual ideas. Quickly draw a series of stick objects, and then choose one to develop. Follow the example described for the letter A. Instead of an ox, your drawing will begin from a sketch of some other ordinary object. You needn't produce an accurate likeness; a simple stick figure will do. Once you have drawn the essentials, rotate and alter the drawing just as the Greeks and Romans did, until you have created a new letterform, distinct from the familiar twenty-six. Simplify its form until you can write it as one more in a string of ordinary letters.

A typographic font is actually composed of many more than twenty-six letters. A complete font includes the capital (sometimes also small capital) and lowercase letters, the numbers (sometimes in an older version with ascenders and descenders, besides the usual aligning figures), all the marks of punctuation, and special characters (such as ñ, ç, and the ligatures æ, fi). Your new letter, as an addition to the complete font, would require both upper- and lowercase versions. You won't need to design both, but decide which case your letter fits best. Then combine it with two or three other letters, at least one of them round and one straight, to form a new word.

Your word is made of simple lines, like the lettering of someone first learning to write. Every letter A has the same underlying structure of lines and space, but each style and school of type creates a different set of clothing for the lines to wear. Typographic design varies the thickness, angle, and terminal flourishes of the strokes, as well as the overall proportions of the letter.

Begin by creating a Gothic suit of clothes for your new word. Study the examples of black-letter type in Figure 4.5. Then, on one line of your lined paper, make several versions of the new word with tightly spaced verticals and angular terminals, using the broad tip of your marker or pencil. Add detail with the fine tip or pen. On each succeeding baseline, make new versions based on the other nonroman styles. Try imitating wedding invitation script, stencils, or a typewriter. Or dress the letters in decorative plumage, Broadway lights, or something more imaginative. Fill one sheet of lined paper with italics, imitatives, decoratives, and black letters to get a feel for these styles.

Then turn to the roman style. Examine the samples of each school of roman type in turn, and on separate lines create versions of your word to match each school. As you work, refer to the following descriptions as well as to previous samples.

For the old style, hold your marker so that the flat edge of the tip tilts slightly (to the right, like the / stroke, called a *virgule* or *solidus*). The angle of the pen produces the stresses in the loops of round strokes and the diagonal serifs on the ascenders of straight strokes. Experiment with different angles, and compare your results with the slow movement away from the diagonal in typographic history. For most old styles, the parts of the letter are broad enough to be inscribed in a circle or square. Outline these shapes.

For the transitional, turn the pen (and shift the paper) so that the flat tip is horizontal to the baseline. Note how the diagonal serifs and stresses disappear (and also how awkward writing may feel, especially for right-handers). Make the thick areas thicker and the thin thinner in these transitionals, but keep the letters broad and round. Add serifs to the bases of the terminal strokes of both old style and transitional letters. Also connect the strokes to the serifs with brackets.

For the modern school, the shapes become more rectangular or oval, the thin areas become hairlines, and the brackets usually disappear. For the square serif, simply reduce the contrast between thin and thick strokes and add thick serifs, and for the sans serif remove the serifs entirely. Spend time studying the specimens and the description for each school and make several tries until these fine distinctions become clear.

Designers also produce several fonts when they create a new typeface. The main version is called *roman*, *book*, or *regular*. Italics (sometimes called *slant* or *oblique*) have become a required font to match most roman typefaces (although some one-of-a-kind or chancery italics are meant to stand alone). There are no precise norms for the weight of boldface, and designers may produce a whole range of weights from thin or light, through demi- and extra-bold, to black. Occasionally a designer includes condensed or expanded/extended versions. These fonts can run the gamut from light italic to extra-bold condensed italic. Univers contains so many variations that the permutations are numbered. Are your own letters bold or slanted? Where would they fit in a complete set of fonts?

Finally, consider the relative size of the letters. Type since the time of Didot has been measured in *points*, a unit that was later standardized in the United States at roughly 1/72 of an inch (about twice the thickness of a human hair). The measurement is not for the letter itself but for the space on which it sits, because type cannot fill its space completely without touching the letters set above and below it. Within that space, the typographic designer has great freedom to make the body of the letters large or small and the ascending and descending strokes long or short. Your design was constrained by the lined paper to have an x-height one-third the size of the total space for each line of type. Did your ascenders and descenders fill the space? Compare the body sizes of the print in Figures 4.5–4.13. Reduced to the same size, would your designs have a large or small x-height?

When type was cast from metal, a different cutting was required for every size. Text or body typography was often prepared in point sizes from 6 through 14. The smaller the size, the more the thin details had to be thickened to hold up under the presses. Display types were cast in the 18-point size and thereafter in multiples of 6 or 12 (24 through 72). The largest sizes, like a banner headline in 144-point Railroad Gothic, were rare and were often set in type cut from wood. Each size then constituted a separate font, but those variations are lost in phototype and digitized type, which simply enlarge or reduce (and may even generate bold or italic versions) from a single font. Using a ruler (you can convert inches to points by dividing by 72), estimate the size of your lettering. How would the design have to change as the font got smaller?

News Typefaces and Modern Design

Although they have been described in relation to the newspaper, the styles and schools of type were traditionally designed for use in books. Early books were valued for their beauty and permanence by collectors, as well as for study and reading by scholars. News periodicals did not publish with regularity until the seventeenth century (Jackson), with the appearance of the *Avisa* and the *Relation* in Germany (although Catich notes that letterers for the Roman government painted daily news on signs). The presentation of miscellaneous news on large sheets of paper began with the *Leipziger Zeitung* and the *London Gazette*, more than two centuries after Gutenberg. With their weekly or daily loose pages of mixed content, newspapers differ utterly from the book, with its permanently bound leaves of flowing text. Although the differences seem obvious, they are frequently ignored by the newspaper publishers, editors, designers, and consultants who make typographic decisions in the twentieth century.

A typical example of ignoring these differences can be found in the *Times* of London (Morison, *Printing*). Until 1799, the *Times*, like most English newspapers of the eighteenth century, used a late old style of Caslon design (Figure 4.17). During the nineteenth century, newspapers in general adopt-

FIGURE 4.17.
Typefaces of
the *Times* of
London.
From a page
showing
Caslon, Old
Roman, and
New Roman
(reduced).
From
Morison
Printing 20
(damaged
original).

PRINTING THE TIMES

These words are composed in a "Monotype" reproduction of the earliest of the group known in the trade as "old face" types. It was first used in 1495. This type was copied all over Europe.

A notable version of this design was cut in France by Claude Garamond.

Garamond's types were copied by the best Dutch cutters who also supplied English printers. The Elzevir editions of the classics carried the Dutch version of the "old-face" design into the favour of London publishers.

———

This is the historic English version known as Caslon Old Face. It was cut about 1720 by William Caslon at the instance of London printers and publishers discontented with continental founts.

John Walter I, founder of *The Times*, purchased the founts for the Logographic Press from Caslon II. Caslon Old Face was used in *The Times* until 1799.

———

This is *The Times* New Roman, designed at Printing House Square expressly for use in *The Times*. The size you are now reading will be used for the principal sections of *The Times*. The several complementary sizes are equally well proportioned for the respective services in the paper. The new fount will be employed on and after October 3, 1932. *The Times*, for generations the best printed paper, will, by present-day optical standards, be the most comfortably readable journal in the world. All the new founts have been tested by the highest ophthalmic authority.

By this adjustment of its columns to the needs of the contemporary reader, *The Times* believes that it is anticipating a general public demand which sooner or later will be made upon journalism at large.

The improvement in the ease of reading may be immediately seen by a comparison of this column with the adjoining matter set in a similar size of the superseded fount.

This specimen of the superseded fount is intended to illustrate, by comparison, the superior legibility of the fount used in the left-hand column. The design of the type used for the composition of these lines originated more than a century ago, when reading habits were different. It is evident that there must be changes in typography as long as our social habits are open to variation. When it was founded, *The Times* was largely read in coffee-houses ; in the nineteenth century it came to be read in trains ; to-day it is largely read in cars and airliners. Reading habits, dependent on social habits, will not remain constant. Neither must newspaper typography remain constant.

Advances in English craftsmanship have now made possible the designing and engraving of the supremely readable fount to be seen in the adjoining column.

The use of the fount in which these words are set will terminate in the issue of *The Times* for October 1, 1932.

ed body typefaces of the modern school crossed with old style and transitional characteristics (Lawson, *Anatomy*). Although these newspaper typefaces printed clearly on low-grade newsprint and held up well under heavy use, they were never much admired or studied by fine typographers.

After the designer Stanley Morison criticized the typography of the *Times*, the publishers hired him in 1929 to revise the newspaper's typography (Moran). His stated goal was to bring the paper up to the standard of "the average book as brought out by London publishers" (Lawson, *Anatomy* 270). The typeface he designed with his collaborator, Victor Lardent, an advertising illustrator at the *Times*, was an old style in structure, but with the narrow letterform widths and the greater contrast of transitionals (Figure 4.17). The new roman reproduced well on the white paper and with the dark ink of the *Times*, which retained the face until 1972. Although Times Roman has become one of the most popular typefaces for books and magazines and is standard on many personal computers, it was never widely adopted by other newspapers, because they use lower-grade newsprint and ink that preclude the high contrast needed for delicate Times design.

Perhaps because he was a typographic historian, in his numerous books and pamphlets Morison became an advocate for the classical movement of typographic design. The classicists sought to revive the typefaces found in Renaissance books, principally of the old style school. One of the metaphors of the movement was set by Beatrice Warde in a 1937 lecture titled "The Crystal Goblet *or* Printing Should Be Invisible." Good drink, Warde argued, would be better appreciated in a clear, fine glass, which reveals the color of the wine, than in an ornate goblet of the most precious metal. The grace and clarity of classical typefaces rendered them invisible, allowing the words and ideas center stage (Figure 4.18).

Morison, Warde, and other classicists were inspired by but also reacted against the work of William Morris (Johnson). They admired the Arts and Crafts movement for reviving interest in design and good craftsmanship. In the 1890s, the Kelmscott Press founded by Morris helped renew the appreciation of fine book work. On the advice of the engraver and printer Emery Walker, he patterned his typefaces after letterforms found in old manuscripts and early printed books. The classicists admired his reverence for tradition and followed his example by drawing on history, but they objected to his choice of a late medieval ideal for typography. The twentieth-century heirs of Morris's medievalism include the private presses in England and the United States. The Village Press of Frederick Goudy printed a few of Goudy's typefaces based on black-letter style.

FIGURE 4.18.
Classical book
school. Page
design, Stanley
Morison, *The
English
Newspaper*
(Cambridge,
Eng.:
Cambridge
UP, 1932).

quarterly, the *Journal of Theological Studies* is unpunctual. Clearly, as the periodicity of a paper is decelerated, its claim to the description 'journal' is reduced; and also, the claim of the writer of a quarterly to the term 'journalist'.

It is an essential condition of the journal that it should be issued with a certain frequency; and that frequency greater than once a year, or once a quarter, or once a month. These yearly, quarterly or monthly measures of frequency may constitute the Periodical, but publication more often than once a month is essential to a Journal. Fortnightly appearance seems not to have become, for any time, a workable term: the conventional measure of frequency within the month has always been the week. English journalism, as to periodicity, started with *weekly* publication. It proceeded through the stages of *twice weekly* and *thrice weekly* to the *daily* (Morning), to the *twice daily* (Morning and Evening). In tracing these stages it is necessary for us first to observe the most characteristic of the styles used by the printers of the news-pamphlets which preceded the newspapers.

§ 1 CORANTOS

HE development of the printed book from the incunable into the much more strictly governed production of the sixteenth century, with the gradual emergence of a consistent typographic aesthetic, is already well known to us. The familiarity of our Elizabethan and Jacobean forefathers with the latter formats inevitably prescribed a book style for 'The Relations'. The News-Books, Intelligencers, Proceedings, Diurnalls and Mercuries of the period from 1622 to 1665, like the earliest form of news relation, conformed to the style of the printed book, or pamphlet. Such a production had its normal text-page, its contents-page, and its title-page.

Thus ' *Newes* concernynge the General Councell Holden at Trydent London Tho Raynalde, 1549,' may well be taken as an early predecessor of the news-book or pamphlet. A later production, dated London 1619, is headed: ' *Newes out of* Holland: Concerning Barnevelt and his fellow-Prisoners,' etc. (cf. Fig. 1). There was published in 1621 (cf. Fig. 2) ' NEWES FROM FRANCE A true Relation . . . of fire in the Citie of Paris,'

Besides classical design, two other twentieth-century movements of typography have influenced newspapers, one based on the functional modernism of the Bauhaus and the New Typography of Jan Tschichold and the other (to be described later in this chapter) based on expressionism. Bauhaus design sought to strip typography to its bare materials and structure.

A single sans-serif alphabet replaced the diversity of traditional typographic materials. Bauhaus designers also rejected the symmetry of classical typography, arguing that an asymmetrical structure for words on the page would best convey beauty and meaning (Tschichold; Ruder). This approach has been summarized in the famous phrase coined by the architect Louis Sullivan, "Form follows function."

The shift to so-called *functional* (that is, modern asymmetrical) newspaper headlines was due largely to the influence of John Allen and the Mergenthaler Linotype Company (Hutt). Allen was a modernist who edited and produced the company's showcase periodical, the *Linotype News*, from a laboratory in Brooklyn. In each issue, he experimented with alternatives to standard headlines. Before the 1920s, most U.S. newspapers used Cheltenham (Hutt), a face of late transitional design that was often set in all capitals, centered or with succeeding lines indented (see Figure 4.15). As commercial and industrial artists adopted a fashion known as *streamlined design*, Allen crusaded for his version of streamlining newspaper headlines. Each issue of the *Linotype News* trumpeted the latest newspaper converted to modernist, flush-left headlines (see Figure 5.5, p. 176).

At issue in the struggle among functionalism, expressionism, and classicism was the power to influence the display and printing of words in the media. The proponents of each movement influenced some fields of design more than others. The classical movement held greatest sway over the design of books throughout the century. Expressionism profoundly affected advertising design. Although functionalism found advocates at newspapers early on, the movement's impact did not become pronounced until fifty years later (see Chapter 5).

Despite the competition, all three movements were branches of twentieth-century modernism (S. Carter). Although they defined craftsmanship and artistry differently and sought to achieve beauty by opposing means, all three movements agreed on the purpose of typography: to convey content.

Classicists used traditional type to avoid interfering with the content, expressionists attempted to enhance the content, and functionalists imposed a severe order to provide a stark backdrop for the content. The relationship between form and content has been a central concern throughout the history of typography.

The Rise of a Science of Legibility

Until the nineteenth century, the knowledge of how type could most effectively convey words was based on the traditions of the craft. Through centuries of experiment, practitioners accumulated an understanding of what made type legible. This knowledge was embedded in the practices handed down from master to apprentice for generations. Industrial changes and the demise of the apprentice system in the nineteenth century threatened the legacy of the past and debased this traditional typographic wisdom. One aim of the revivalist mentality of the late nineteenth and early twentieth centuries was the restoration of typographic knowledge.

The modernist movements of the twentieth century continued to fill the gap created by the degradation of traditional knowledge about type, readability, and typographic design. But the process took a particular turn at newspapers, where journalists looked to science and scientific inquiry to guide typographic decisions. Newspaper design was more amenable to scientific control than other publication genres have been, for reasons that derive from the practices and institutions of journalism. Newspaper editors and reporters engage in a search for factual truth that has affinities with the goals of empirical science. The economic pressures of manufacturing a product daily or weekly also encouraged a commitment to science, which was considered more efficient than the slow accretion of traditional knowledge.

The new science of legibility began by measuring how

letters were perceived and comparing how different designs were read. (The former measure is called *legibility*, the latter *readability*, but the two terms are used interchangeably here.) In 1926, R. L. Pyke published a *Report on the Legibility of Print*, which initiated a program of scientific experiments. Pyke began by surveying contradictory results from the scattered investigations of printers, advertisers, publishers, psychologists, ophthalmologists, and physiologists of the previous century.

You should always believe all you read in the newspaper, as this makes them more interesting.

— *Rose Macauley*

These studies of legibility began in the 1790s, when the French Imprimerie Nationale asked a panel of expert judges to read type samples at various distances to compare the new modern typeface of Didot with the old style Garamond, which was found to be readable at a greater range of distances. In the 1820s, Charles Babbage reported that the aligning figures were more legible for scientific instruments than the numbers with ascenders and descenders. Both of these conclusions were contradicted by later research. Beginning in 1878, Emile Javal's controlled experiments revealed that the reading eye moves in a series of jumps across the page (he called these *saccadic movements*) and that the upper half of letters is more legible than the lower half. From these results, Javal proposed that typefaces be redesigned without descenders.

A current reading of Pyke's exhaustive survey of early experiments reveals several patterns. First, legibility research may tend to increase during periods of typographic change, when an older style is under assault. Although the goal of the research is usually to find essential truth, the results tend to reflect the customs and practices of the time, familiar to the investigators and study participants. In the French experiment, for example, the experts who found Didot less readable were typographers trained to use Garamond. Legibility study grew over the course of the nineteenth and twentieth centuries, to match the frenzied turns of stylistic fashion, which were encouraged by changes in technology and industry.

Another pattern apparent in Pyke's report is that early results often are contradicted by later studies, not only as measurements become more sophisticated but also as customs change. Only in the realm of physiological measurements, such as saccadic movements, do concrete observations remain relatively unchanged, but these are without many practical uses in typographic design or selection. For example, no one has taken seriously Javal's proposals to shear off the bottoms of letters.

From his own experiments, Pyke found that only extremely large differences in type produced any differences in legibility. He concluded that readers find most legible whatever type they are accustomed to and that the measurement of "objective legibility must be almost impossible" (Pyke 60). Despite the difficulty, he combed his own and others' research to find this universal standard: The ideal letters for reading body text should be fairly simple, broad, and thick, without extreme contrast. His description seems to suggest that the average, middling, and least distinctive faces are the most legible.

Allen of the *Linotype News* and his followers in American journalism responded enthusiastically to the new science of legibility, which inspired at least a dozen typefaces specifically created for newspapers (Spencer, *Visible*). What the so-called legibility types designed by twentieth-century typefounders (Figure 4.19) have in common is the fairly broad, thick letters and unexaggerated contrast recommended by Pyke. The Mergenthaler Linotype Company introduced the first of the group, Ionic, in 1926, based on a square-serif of the Clarendon design. Three more faces—Excelsior, Opticon, and Paragon—were released in the 1930s, followed in 1941 by Corona, the body face recently in use at roughly half of all newspapers. Linotype's chief competitor, Intertype, issued Ideal in 1928 (in response to Ionic), followed in 1935 by

FIGURE 4.19.
Legibility
types. Selected
specimen type-
faces, *Specimen
Book: Linotype
Faces* (Brooklyn:
Mergenthaler
Linotype, n.d.),
and *Supplement:
New Faces*
(1948).

7-POINT IONIC NO. 5

How is one to assess and evaluate a
type face in terms of its esthetic design? Why do the pace-makers in the
art of printing rave over a specific
face of type? What do they see in it?
Why is it so superlatively pleasant to
their eyes?

7-POINT NO. 1 EXCELSIOR

How is one to assess and evaluate a
type face in terms of its esthetic design? Why do the pace-makers in the
art of printing rave over a specific
face of type? What do they see in it?
Why is it so superlatively pleasant to
their eyes?

7-POINT OPTICON

How is one to assess and evaluate
a type face in terms of its esthetic
design? Why do the pace-makers in
the art of printing rave over a specific face of type? What do they see
in it? Why is it so superlatively
pleasant to their eyes?

7-POINT PARAGON

How is one to assess and evaluate
a type face in terms of its esthetic
design? Why do the pace-makers in
the art of printing rave over a specific face of type? What do they see
in it? Why is it so superlatively
pleasant to their eyes?

7-POINT CORONA WITH ERBAR
BOLD

How is one to assess and evaluate a typ
of its esthetic design? Why do the pace
art of printing rave over a specific face
do they see in it? Why is it so superla
to their eyes? **Good design is always pr**
And what they see in a good type desig
excellent practical fitness to perform i

(all specimens 1-point leaded)

Regal, the typeface de-
signed for the *Chicago
Tribune,* and then by Rex,
created for the *Milwaukee
Journal* in 1939. A 1957
design, Imperial, was
adopted in 1967 by the
New York Times, and a
fifth Intertype "legibility"
face, Royal, was intro-
duced in 1960 (to com-
pete with Linotype's
Corona). These faces all
fall within the later transitional school (Lawson,
Anatomy).

Throughout the cen-
tury, Pyke's successors
continued to refine the
approach to measuring
legibility. Their defini-
tions and methods were
usually behaviorist and
relied on electrical
equipment (such as the
tachistoscope, an appara-
tus that measures per-
ception and speed by
exposing words for short,
precise periods of time),
but they disagreed over
what to measure. In the
1930s and the 1940s,
Matthew Luckiesh advo-
cated a method that
counted blinking as a

sign of reading discomfort. His studies were attacked by fellow scientists such as Donald Patterson and Miles Tinker of the University of Minnesota, who preferred to record reading speed.

Both methods contributed to the emerging profile of the behavior of the average eye. By the 1960s, researchers had measured the average rate of reading (250 to 300 words per minute), the average reading distance (12–14 inches), the average range of focus (4 letters in the central area in sharpest focus, called the *fovea*, and 8–11 in the peripheral zone), and other measures such as the average fixation pause between saccadic movements and the average rate of regressions (jumping back before continuing ahead), as well as the effects of content, light, paper, and typography on these averages.

It is always the unreadable that occurs.

— Oscar Wilde

The legacy of legibility research has been to document several general observations about typography, many of them long understood within the craft: Capital letters and italics are harder to read than plain small letters. Darker or bolder letters are usually easier to read. Tinted backgrounds have a negligible effect on reading. Dark letters on light paper are easier to read than light letters of the same size reversed from a dark background. Extremely long or short lines of type slow reading by requiring more regression movements or fixation pauses. And justified type (aligned on both sides) is no more legible than ragged or unjustified type (summarized by Rehe).

Unlike craft-based knowledge, these research findings too often acquire the status of immutable laws. But they cannot succeed as design caveats for two reasons. First, the results come from controlled environments that have little relation to the real-world practice of reading. By changing the lighting, the position of reading, and the angle of the paper, readers exert as much control over legibility as any factor researchers measure. The studies not only fail to allow for variable reading conditions, they also do not measure the levels of reader motivation. Although few use a magnifying glass, investors, sports fans, bargain hunters, and others equally committed to specific content routinely read type that breaks all putative laws of legibility. Controlled experiments also ignore the social interactions and ordinary distractions that may impinge on the reader's commitment.

Second, the results aspire to essential truths or universal standards for what in fact are mutable, social practices. At best, the rules indicate what is common, popular, and familiar at a given moment in the sweep of stylistic change. But the authority of science introduces a rigidity, a resistance to innovation. As a tool for marketing products to specific audiences, legibility rules may contribute to a predictable standardization. Guided by their knowledge of the craft, designers routinely break rules, pushing the limits to establish new styles. The small type tightly letterspaced on long, widely spaced lines that is now in fashion in magazines may not have been scientifically legible when first introduced, but it could soon become so.

Consequences of Legibility Science

Legibility researchers have often produced specific results showing that one school or face is superior to another. Just as old style was once found to be more readable than modern, both were recently considered more readable than sans serif. These results usually don't hold up as styles change. Some researchers have tried to avoid the uncertainty of shifting styles by searching for firm ground in an optimal set of specifications. For example, Patterson and Tinker said the ideal book should among other things be set in 11-point type. In 1963, Tinker recommended longer lines (that is, wider columns), more leading between lines, and 8- or 9-point type sizes for newspapers.

149

Even these general ideals show how little legibility scientists have understood either the measurement of type or the meaning of the typographic craft. The visual sizes of different typefaces can vary greatly for the same point size. A better gauge of type size might be the height of the lowercase letters exclusive of ascenders and descenders, most easily seen in the small *x*. A large x-height makes 9-point Helvetica dramatically larger to the eye than 9-point Garamond, which has a smaller x-height with long ascenders and descenders. Such variance makes size specifications of legibility research only vaguely meaningful. No standard unit of x-height has ever been established, and even if it were, the variable length of ascenders and descenders would render it of little practical value.

Although the specifications of legibility science fall short as a practical guide, the research did document the changes in newspaper text sizes (Tinker). Late-nineteenth-century newspapers commonly used 6-point body type. Although the first "legibility" type was nominally 6 1/2-point, the recommendations of research produced an x-height closer to a typical 8-point type, so that fewer letters fit on the line than the half-point change seemed to imply. By the 1930s, 7-point body had become common, and, in part because of legibility science, 8- and 8 1/2-point were standard by the late 1950s. Recently, twice as many newspapers were using 9-point as 8 1/2-point type. Because of the size of the x-height, these types continue to appear larger than their nominal sizes might imply.

The consequences of these changes were more than cosmetic; they had profound implications for journalism (Barnhurst). From 1885 to 1985, the number of words that would fit on the typical front page fell from 12,000 to 4,400 (Barnhurst and Nerone). The number of pages in the newspaper increased, but so did the amount of space used for pictures, headlines, and everything else but body text. It is safe to say that a great deal of what once could fit on the front page had to move inside, ended up unpublished as overset type, or never got reported at all.

The role of legibility research in this process is clear. Researchers tested reading speed to find the optimal typeface, size, line length, and leading. These objective measures generally coincided with the stated preferences of the study participants. All else being equal, they opined, larger sizes and wider columns with more leading make for faster, more comfortable reading. But all else was not and cannot be equal. A spacious, large-type newspaper must exclude something. A given reader might want whatever catches his or her particular interest displayed that way, even as somebody else's interest gets pushed aside, off the front pages or out of the newspaper entirely.

Reduced coverage on the front page, where it matters, narrows the audience whose particular interests can be covered there and reduces the chances for creating new interests. As newspapers seek to attract more readers, the use of large type becomes a structural barrier to diversity. Although it might be slower to read, a tighter front page could serve a more diverse audience and reward minority coverage. As readers found more groups treated prominently, including their own, they might identify more strongly with the newspaper. In other words, a moderate reduction in conventional legibility could in fact increase readership. Even if it failed to do so, the change would signal the newspaper's commitment to a civic, rather than merely commercial, agenda.

Larger type not only reduced the coverage on the front page but also tied the newspaper to particular ways of reading and groups of readers. The largest body type, a 12-point size called *primer*, is linked to juvenile readers. Conventional practice since the nineteenth century has connected primer type to school readers and picture books for children, even though research in the 1960s found that the smaller the child, the smaller the legible type (Swann). The next largest body type, commonly referred to as *large print*, is linked to older readers. Large-print Bibles and "senior-citizen" printed ephemera have set the conventional significance of these type sizes. Small type, set 8-point or smaller, is linked to assiduous, devoted readers. It is used conventionally in the fine print of contracts and reference works. By shifting from fine print to large print, newspapers abandoned their visual role as a compendium, favoring instead the typographic dress of leisure and retirement. Except in classifieds and in business and sports statistics, the signs of the poring and culling aficionado of news were replaced by the signs of comfort and convenience that signify either the older or the casual, uncommitted reader.

🙰 Many other factors came to bear in this process. American publishers for some time have been aware that the U.S. population is aging. Older readers take more time to read and are among the most loyal of newspaper subscribers. Enlarging the type seemed to serve an important, primary audience for the medium. Publishers have also recognized that larger type can help the bottom line. If fewer words can fit on a page, then fewer need be researched, written, typeset, and printed. Profit, however, was probably of secondary concern. Enlarging the type size seemed to provide a way of serving readers while simultaneously saving money. Everyone appeared to benefit. But publishers and legibility researchers made a fundamental miscalculation.

> *It* is the newspaper's duty to print news and raise hell.
> — *Wilbur F. Storey*

Adopting the visual signs of leisure activity and older readers aligned the medium with a narrowing audience. As leisure time declines, the newspaper-as-leisure must compete for readers' free time. A quick and easy design requires relaxed contents, not the hard stuff of documenting community life and assisting with the chores of adulthood and the duties of citizenship. Leisurely content in turn makes the newspaper optional, just another recreational outlet among many. The aging population might seem to promise some respite, but only temporarily. Newspapers cannot survive without a constant infusion of young readers, who are the least likely to adopt a form clearly marked with the signs of advancing age (Barnhurst and Wartella).

These consequences for the content of the newspaper and the meaning of its typographic form are only partly due to legibility science. The researchers were also participating in the style of their times. Pyke, who lived in an era that could not accept sans-serif type in text, disregarded his own finding that plain typefaces were more legible. When Tinker, who worked in a period enamored of all things large and spacious (described in Chapter 5), found that 7-point type was just as legible as 8-point, he still called for larger sizes. Recent research on justified columns recommended setting type ragged, despite its own findings that neither justified nor ragged type had significantly better legibility. These recommendations spring not strictly from the data but in no small measure from the prevailing visual style. A concern for content and for consequences might have led newspapers in quite a different direction, perhaps to smaller, sans-serif body type.

Typographic Expressionism

The consequences of form were a central concern of the modernist typographic craft, classicist as well as functionalist. The *expressionists* insisted that type should magnify and even exaggerate the content. They were inspired by the unfettered typographic experiments of the Futurist and Dada movements (Figure 4.20), as well as by expressionist and, later, surreal art. Emilio Marinetti, who authored the Futurist manifesto published in *Le Figaro* in 1909, opposed "what is known as the harmony of setting. When necessary, we shall use . . . twenty different type faces. We shall represent hasty perceptions in *italic* and express a **scream** in **bold** type. . . ." (quoted in Spencer, *Pioneers* 17). Along with their discovery of beauty in industrial forms, the Futurists embraced the implications of a display typography originating in advertising and associated with a commercial press.

Expressionism coincided with the rise of another strain of scientific inquiry, *congeniality research* (summarized by Zachrisson). In the 1870s, psychologists began to study the correspondence between content and typographic form. In the 1920s and 1930s, various researchers, including Gestalt psychologists, investigated the moods invoked by typefaces. The field saw a resurgence in the 1960s, when cognitive psychologists and mass-communication researchers began to use semantic techniques to measure the meanings of type. The research generally confirmed the craft-based lore of expressionist typographers, which not only equated bold typefaces with strength but also tied italics to speed and delicacy, sans serifs to plainness, and the like.

FIGURE 4.20. Futurist experimental typography. Book cover, Filippo T. Marinetti, *Futurist Manifesto*, 1915 (Ex Libris, New York).

154

Although these studies tested for an objective code of typographic connotations, they are interesting today for the attitudes they reveal among researchers and typographers and for the insights they provide into changing styles. The studies noted that typographers made stronger, more elaborated judgments of type than did readers (Brinton). What the researchers failed to recognize was their informants' craft-based knowledge of styles and periods. Despite the severe limitations of the experimental setting, typographers still managed to show whether the faces were fashionable or not and to indicate their historical significance.

The meanings assigned to type by readers and typographers seem to spring not from some objective code but from the cultural experience common to both groups. Early studies were most concerned with such perceived qualities as strength, warmth, and dignity (Ovink). During the 1960s, the concept of strength was transmogrified into ruggedness and potency, terms with gender connotations. The whole research enterprise expanded its concern for differentiating the masculine from the feminine (e.g., Kastl and Child). Some cursive and frilly typefaces were overtly identified as expressing feminine qualities, while a tacit interest in masculine forms increased. These changes reveal not only the fluctuating cultural meanings of type but also the tendency of expression to feed on stereotypes.

The expressionist movement gained momentum in the editorial side of newspapers, primarily on feature pages, where designers trained in art schools began to use type as an image, not only conveying but also illustrating words (Figure 4.21). Letterforms had appeared as labels and legends in medieval painting but disappeared in art after the Renaissance. The Cubist movement early in the twentieth century reintegrated letterforms into painting, not as captions and labels but as apparently real elements within their images. Picasso and Braque did not greatly influence typographers, but the Futurists attempted to make typographic printing a more direct expression of its times. As newspapers moved first to phototype and more recently to computer type, the letterforms could be stretched, enlarged, and scattered across the page at will, and the use of type as expressive form expanded.

Expressionist typography draws on several sources of meaning (Elam). One of the most common is the allusion to periods of history and style. The typography of any era invokes contemporary values and tastes. When the content of an article or text shares the values identified with that era, typography selected from the same period will amplify the content. Another common source of typographic meaning is found in references to physical objects or images. In a sort of visual onomatopoeia, the form of typography can mimic sizes, weights, shapes, and postures from the environment. Large, bold headlines are mimetic of dramatic events. In whimsical feature articles, letterforms might take the shape of ghosts, cooking utensils, or hairdos. This typography, itself becoming an image that imitates the content of a text, is thought to extend the meaning of content. A third common source of expressionist meaning is the use of visual puns and double meanings. Typography that breaks conventional rules takes on another sense. When the word *CO°LD* headlines

FIGURE 4.21. Type as image. Poster-style page, *Virginian-Pilot* and *Ledger-Star* [Norfolk] 21 Dec. 1989: C1. Rpt. in *Eleventh Edition: Best of Newspaper Design* (Reston: SND, 1990) 215.

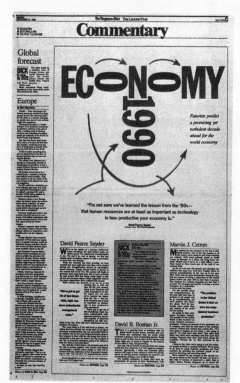

FIGURE 4.22.
Type as mean-
ing. Banner
headline, *New
York Post* 5
Aug. 1938: 1.
Rpt. in
*America's Front
Page News*, ed.
Michael C.
Emery, R.
Smith
Schuneman,
and Edwin
Emery (New
York:
Doubleday,
1970) 252.

FIGURE 4.23.
Type with
double mean-
ing. *Chicago
Sun-Times* 19
Dec. 1963: 1.

FIGURE 4.24.
Type as
expression.
*Left: Boston
Herald
American* 31
Mar. 1979: 1.
*Right: Boston
Herald
American* 26
Jan. 1980: 1.

a weather story, the two letters O double as *zero degrees*. Turning a word upside-down can suggest the state of the world. When the new sense and the content of the text coincide (Figures 4.22–4.24), meaning may be reinforced or expanded.

The difficulty with expressionist typography is that it can quickly descend into cliché. Some newspaper designs reduce expressionism to a stock of ethnic or national stereotypes (Craig, "Aesthetics" and "Designing"). The rich history of typographic development can become a series of markers for racial groups — Celtic, Germanic, and such vague and potentially offensive categories as "Oriental." Some newspaper design textbooks have approvingly identified typefaces with specific nationalities (Figure 4.25), mostly European — for example, Bodoni with Italians, Garamond with the French, and Caslon with English. The emphasis on gender in the 1950s and 1960s led newspapers to adopt "feminine" cursives and italics for the women's page and blocky sans serifs and square serifs for sports pages.

If these clichés are avoided, typography can extend the means of expression in journalism. Editors and perhaps even reporters can draw on recent typographic movements for options in the presentation of display and body text, by enhancing (or possibly contradicting for ironic effect) the meaning of the content or by seeking to make the typography invisible or neutral. Some linguists have suggested that typography is a sort of macro-punctuation, which has begun entering the vernacular just as punctuation developed in the Middle Ages.

FIGURE 4.25. Type as cultural cliché. Roy Paul Nelson, *Publication Design* (Dubuque: Brown, 1983) 79.

GREECE
JAMAICA
Ceylon
China
MEXICO
Tahiti
Canada
Ireland
Scotland
𝔇enmark
Japan
ꝐORꞆUGꞀL
BRITAIN

The spread of microcomputers with typographic capabilities can put the means of expression into more hands. Not without irony, computers born of industrial technology have begun to transport publishing back to the chaotic era before Charlemagne, when those with the minds, means, and muscle could make and use letterforms in manuscript books. Stanley Morison has said that entirely new typographic styles and schools depended on innovations in handwriting and calligraphy (Morison and Jackson). But the computer may be mightier than the pen (see Figure 5.15, p. 198). Newspapers have the power to impose standards and encourage new styles.

The danger is that editors might make typographic decisions that promote the interests of the privileged few and stereotype the rest. A better alternative is for journalists to enlarge tolerance and civility through typography. Such good manners can be accomplished only through sustained effort. When choosing a typeface, editors and publishers should carefully review its history and recent use, exploring its denotations and larger connotations. The advice of external consultants and results of scientific studies must be filtered critically, so that local customs and peculiarities do not get overruled. Any study of the newspaper's audience should include groups in the circulation area who have not previously been readers.

Newspapers cannot simply ignore the shifting currents of style, but editors can pay close attention to the ways in which new styles affect the content of the newspaper. Attention to strict rules of legibility is probably much less important than using type to encourage broader, more inclusive coverage. Finally, a knowledge of the craft—the customs and rules of typography—should promote not a slavish traditionalism but a new freedom. In the struggle between personal action and social convention, journalists need to experiment and explore, learning the rules if only to break them intelligently.

CHAPTER 5

When I first began to work in the graphic arts, the people I

knew had never heard of such a job. They had a notion of

*E*VALUATING

what writers do from personal experience, and they under-

LAYOUT

stood the role of printers. For several years, my parents kept

asking me to explain what I did exactly and, when introduc-

ing me to their friends, would stumble for a job title. I first

tried to explain my work with an assembly line analogy: The

writer puts the ideas into words, the graphic artist puts the words into type, and the printer puts the type into pages. Oh, they said, you're a typographer? Well, not exactly.

Eventually, I hit on a minimalist answer that seemed cryptic enough to scuttle the conversation: I was an arranger of rectangles. So-called modular layout was the rage at the time, combined with the severe Swiss school of typography, a graphics version of the boxy glass towers from International Style architecture. Because type was not an issue (we all pledged allegiance to Helvetica) and color was still a luxury, the central concern of graphics was the arrangement of visual space.

𝒩ews expands to fill the time and space allotted to its coverage.

— *William Safire*

🖾 At professional conferences, stories of identity problems were second only to how-I-stumbled-into-design stories. My own difficulty was solved when I became a teacher, something everyone readily understood. But within twenty years, graphics had become a commonplace. People began to wear logos and typography on T-shirts and to argue about a politician's "image." Over the same period, newspapers not only introduced color, added more charts, and changed typography, but also followed a succession of fashions in layout (Barnhurst, "News"). It seemed to my generation of graphic artists that a revolution had taken place (Gentry and Zang). Instead of feigning polite interest, people really knew and cared about our work. Instead of stumbling into a job, students planned to follow our career.

A revolution requires an explanation: What exactly happened? What were the causes? How did things change? What did it mean? In articles and textbooks, the newspaper design revolution is divided into two periods: the *modern* (or "contemporary"), for what newspapers do today, and the *traditional*, for everything that went before (e.g., Click and Stempel). In the standard explanation, outside forces such as governmental authority and industrial machinery determined the appearance of the traditional newspaper, whereas in the modern period functional and optimal designs have prevailed (e.g., Baird, McDonald, Pittman, and Turnbull). Technological advances and competition from other media in the marketplace seem to spur the progression from traditional to modern design.

The histories we graphic artists tell about the newspaper seem to point ultimately toward a future in which the newspaper will cease to exist in any substantially recognizable form. Innovators and leading designers predict that newspapers will be largely replaced by paperless devices connected to electronic networks and designed to look more or less like magazines (American Press Institute). These prognostications, accompanied by a weakening base of advertisers and young readers, put the newspaper form at grave risk.

Yet scholars and critics have not questioned the standard version of events. This chapter delivers a broadside against the received rendering of newspaper design history, in which graphic artists are their own invention, unlike anything that went before. It examines critically the common assumptions of the field—for example, that modern design rests on timeless scientific foundations. Finally, it aims to provoke a response to the newspaper as a visual form and a cultural artifact. By viewing skeptically our claims to authority, journalists and critical readers may help graphic artists to imagine alternatives to the current standards of layout and to envision a future that still has room for newspapers.

A Received History of Newspaper Design

The received history of newspaper design had its first telling in the writing of John E. Allen. Allen's purpose was polemical: to refute the principles controlling traditional newspaper design and replace them with the modernism he demonstrated on the pages of the *Linotype News*. His success can be measured in the more or less complete dominance of his version of history in all the subsequent accounts. These are found principally in the practitioner literature, the professional handbooks and university textbooks used to train journalists and graphic artists (described in Barnhurst, "News"). Allen's dispute with traditional layout has also filtered into the academy, where it set the agenda for research on newspaper design (summarized in Barnhurst and Nerone).

The visual appearance of newspapers plays only a marginal role in other histories of the medium. Frank Luther Mott's *American Journalism* makes passing and inconsistent references to visual details. These are even more scarce in recent social histories (e.g., Schudson). The problem is only partly redressed in the compilations of historic front pages (e.g., Emery; Jones) and in illustrated histories (e.g., Williams). Reproduced images and the facts of trim sizes and typefaces cannot substitute for argument (Nerone). There are few book-length histories of the field (Manevy; Morison, *English* and *Origins*), and the only widely distributed volume, written by Allen Hutt, an admirer and junior colleague of John Allen, adopts the modernist polemic. Although the literature is meager, the facts collected by these and writers such as Harold Evans can support other explanations besides those handed down since the 1930s.

According to that received history, the newspaper form came about almost entirely by accident. The early printer-publishers looked to turn a profit by serving the public's interest in current events. Their strategy was to employ an existing investment in book-printing equipment to reproduce news of public occurrences by the cheapest means (Chappell). The visual appearance of their product and service was supposedly a matter of little concern. Later, various pressures from government, advertisers, circulation, and the news itself combined to demand a series of technical innovations that further altered the newspaper. By the end of the nineteenth

FIGURE 5.1.
Comparison of
newspaper
formats,
1645–1829.
Frontispiece in
Morison,
English.

century, the traditional newspaper had fully emerged. It was the large, bawling brat of technology, its scruffy appearance less the product of design than of sheer inattention.

In this version of history, design practitioners and journalism educators typically describe the development of three aspects of the newspaper's layout (aside from attending to body typography, covered in its own chapter): the notably large dimensions of some newspaper formats, the typographically distinct headlines, and the ordering or ranking of the stories in the make-up of the page. Each of these aspects is thought to have emerged from technology under the pressure of various economic forces.

The most cited aspect of this history is format—how newspapers became peculiarly large (Figure 5.1). In 1712, the British Parliament imposed a duty on paper, which continued in effect until 1855. Other levies on printing and advertising (including the Stamp Acts notorious in U.S. history) led English publishers to economize by using a large sheet instead of several smaller ones. During the nineteenth century, formats got even larger. Mechanized papermaking, invented by the Fourdrinier family and put into operation in 1803, allowed for sheets larger than could be made by hand. Lord Stanhope's invention of the iron press in 1800 made possible a larger impression than could be made on wooden presses. Mechanization was driven by the growth in news coverage and in circulation.

Headlines twice the size of events.

— *John Galsworthy*

The received history follows the same tack when describing the origins of newspaper headlines. In the early nineteenth century, some American newspapers are said to have set their nameplates in black letter because it was the only large type readily available on the frontier. In the United States and Europe, larger and more varied headline typefaces met the exigencies of news. Revolutions, civil wars, and international conflicts grew in intensity from the eighteenth to the twentieth centuries, increasing the need for urgent-looking typography. At the same time, advertisers demanded stronger and more varied display, providing a haphazard array of type in display sizes.

According to this version of history, the use of larger, bolder headlines was limited by the strictures of available machinery. Revolving presses, which rotated the type to make successive impressions on individual sheets of paper, were introduced at newspapers in the 1840s. To prevent the type from flying out of the rotating print drum, column rules running the height of the page wedged the type in place. These column dividers are thought to have made headlines of more than one column impossible. As a result, events until the turn of the nineteenth century were headlined with a series of stacked titles called *decks*. The New York *Sun* reported the outbreak of the U.S. Civil War at Fort Sumter with ten decks, and the *Chicago Tribune* ran fifteen decks in a single column after the Chicago fire.

The received history follows a similar pattern to explain the origins of newspaper make-up. The first newspapers are said to have been a jumble of miscellaneous correspondence and reports from the post and from arriving ships. Early printer-publishers merely poured these contents haphazardly into pages that were styled after the book. As pages got larger and headlines emerged, printers continued to fill in the columns from top to bottom, beginning from the left and ignoring the mass of gray type that inevitably flooded the bottom of the page. The column rules that limited headlines likewise kept page make-up in a rigidly vertical mold, even after newspaper printing became completely separated from the book trade.

The Myths of Layout

Although the events and conditions of this received history are for the most part reported accurately, their significance to newspaper layout may be exaggerated. Through frequent retelling, they seem to have taken on mythic proportions. The ebbs and flows in newspaper format are seen as a consequence of governmental regulations, technical innovations, and the growth of news as a product, an occupation, and a pastime. The facts of the narrative are not in dispute; taxes were imposed, circulation and coverage grew, machines were invented, and newspapers got larger. But the causal link between events and the newspaper format seems to be overstated.

The British tax on paper did not initiate relatively large newspaper formats. Early printed and manuscript news sheets were often large to begin with, closer in size to today's magazines than to most novels. A full sheet of book paper (roughly 25 by 38 inches) folded in half two times produces a magazine-sized format called a *quarto*, for the four leaves (eight pages) that result. Folded one more time, the sheet produces a book-sized format called an *octavo*. After the paper tax was imposed, some English octavo newspapers grew to the quarto size that had been common in early European news sheets.

> *This folio of four pages, happy work!*
>
> — *William Cowper*

Other taxes, on advertisements published and on newspaper copies printed, were irrelevant to any changes in format. In the United States, the Stamp Acts had a symbolic importance, inspiring independence-minded protests in 1765 over the issue of taxation and representation, but their effect on the size of newspapers was nil. Nor did subsequent local taxes favor one format over another. The large newspaper became standard in the United States at the end of the eighteenth century, well after the English taxes had been removed.

During the nineteenth century, newspaper formats are said to have come under the sway of technology. Power-driven and later rotary presses working from rolls or "webs" of paper and the introduction of wood-pulp newsprint in the 1870s get attention in most accounts, although these inventions did not in themselves alter newspaper layout. Other technical innovations did make larger formats possible. The huge blanket sheets of several New York newspapers at mid-century could not have been published without large presses. The *Morning Courier and New-York Enquirer* reached 27 by 32 1/2 inches in the 1850s. The single issue of the *Illuminated Quadruple*

FIGURE 5.2.
Book-style
layout.
London
Diurnall, no.
45, 24 Apr.
1643: 1. From
Hutt 12.

Constellation, published on July 4, 1859, had thirteen columns on a 35-by-50-inch page. These extreme examples play prominently in most accounts, clearly indicating the foregrounding of technology, even though they were little more than publicity stunts.

The headlines peculiar to the newspaper are said to have originated partly from inattention — a willingness to make do with whatever was handy — and partly from editorial and mechanical necessity. Once again, the story is nominally accurate. Some early newspapers did resemble books. Wars took place, circulation increased, and newspaper headlines changed. Advertising typography grew larger and more varied. Type-revolving presses required column rules, deck headlines emerged, and vertical make-up persisted. But the events did not alone necessitate the adoption of any one form of layout.

Strong headlines originated before the nineteenth century. Among the earliest news sheets, individual reports were labeled, in some cases with distinct and attention-getting typography. In addition to titles in italics, in boldface, and in all capital letters, some newspapers in the seventeenth century introduced each story with a shoulder heading, set in the margin beside the column of body text (see Figure 5.2). The surrounding space set off all these summary titles, making them as visually distinct as many headlines that came later. Newspapers also used large initial letters, bold ruled lines, and woodcut devices that stood in sharp contrast with the surrounding body text to mark the beginnings of stories. These early newspapers had as much typographic variety of weight, spacing, and arrangement as many of their descendants. They introduced the elements that later flourished in the deck headlines of the nineteenth century, including the custom of summarizing the story in several lines of centered typography distinct from the text.

*H*armony seldom makes a headline.

— *Silas Bent*

🕮 Nor did the pressures from news events or advertising necessarily cause headlines to change. Many newspapers continued to use small labels and titles to cover the various nineteenth-century wars, suggesting that increased war coverage was capable of crowding headlines as well as expanding them. Likewise, larger advertising display may have been as likely to urge economies in headline space as to encourage large headlines.

Upon closer inspection, the technical barrier to multicolumn headlines does not turn out to be nearly as impermeable as it is credited with being. Very few American newspapers installed type-revolving presses, and within a decade many of these had begun stereotyping. This innovation—the process of taking a flexible papier-mâché mold of the type and then casting a curved plate for printing—removed the limitations of type-revolving printing. Although the technical practices at large U.S. newspapers are supposed to be the source of the conventional one-column headlines, these papers ran two-column headlines (and advertisements) before stereotyping by simply setting the words with the column rule running between the letters. Whatever the role of technology in the process, other explanations must be found for the fact that in England, for example, the first multicolumn headline did not appear until 1895.

Newspaper page make-up is also said to have originated from a certain inattention to design, but this assumption seems inaccurate. The earliest English newspaper publishers

FIGURE 5.3.
Conventional
newspaper
form, 1797.
*Porcupine's
Gazette*
[Philadelphia]
5 Sept. 1797:
1. Rpt. in
Barnard Fay,
*Notes on the
American Press
at the End of the
Eighteenth
Century* (New
York: Grolier,
1927) 15.

FIGURE 5.4.
Conventional
newspaper
form, 1880.
*The Tombstone
Epitaph*
[Arizona] 31
July 1880: 1.
Rpt. in *The
Story of America
as Reported by
Its Newspapers,
1690–1965*,
ed. Edwin
Emery (New
York: Simon,
1965) 91.

took intense interest in the ordering of news, collecting related materials together, presenting "broken stuffe," or news
briefs, summarizing and tabulating the points in parliamentary
debate and the items in shipping, and placing as many principal "relations" or stories as possible on the first news page,
along with a listing of other contents. All of these techniques
originated within the first twenty-five years of newspaper
publishing in Britain (Steinberg).

Newspapers did begin with the first column and fill in the
others across the page. Although reading matter flowed from
top to bottom within each column, the dominant direction
for all the columns, and for the page as a whole, was from left
to right. The arrangement was every bit as intelligible as, and
even more sequential than, any subsequent style of make-up.
Individual items were immediately distinguishable because of
the gaps in text matter as well as the title typography. To read
the gray at the bottom of the page as evidence of inattention
misses the structure of the page.

Each of the influences on newspaper layout cited as crucial
in the received history turns out to be less than persuasive
under close scrutiny. Most accounts buttress these particular
influences by arguing that newspapers have been extremely
conservative in their approach to layout. Changes, once

imposed by outside forces, are thought to become part of a self-perpetuating tradition (Figures 5.3 and 5.4). However, newspaper conservatism has shown great power to resist the very forces said to have motivated layout changes. During the period of the most rapid mechanization, in the late nineteenth century, newspapers changed little in appearance. The mythic events retold in the received history may provide a partial explanation for the origins of newspaper design, but other influences were probably of equal or greater significance.

Beyond the Foundational Myths

Amid all the attention to taxes, wars, advertising, and especially technology, the received history of newspaper layout and design all but ignores the importance of changing styles and conventions. Newspapers have throughout their history engaged in a complex dialogue with the prevailing culture. A large format, for instance, has traditionally carried greater authority than a small format in publishing conventions. Manuscript books set the pattern long before the invention of printing. Great folio volumes were held by universities for serious study, but portable octavo books eventually found a place as light reading, in pockets or on nightstands (Chartier). Both history and practice assigned meaning to the form of books, and newspaper publishers responded to established genres. The technology of printing followed, rather than directed, the prevailing custom.

Journalism balances authority with popular appeal, and the form of newspapers guides on those opposing poles. In the seventeenth century, newspaper design reflected the styles of the popular forms of communication. Besides the book, another important influence on newspaper design was correspondence—handwritten letters that traditionally have carried private news. Although expensive, manuscript newsletters circulated among subscribers in England until the early eighteenth century. When Ichabod Dawks converted his newsletter to print in 1695, he had a typeface cut to imitate the handwritten version. As newspapers copied from existing formats, they also altered them. The octavo format of books was adapted to display the mixed content of news. The aspects of headlines and make-up described changed and adjusted the conventions of book design for the purposes of the new medium.

An emphasis on tax policies in the eighteenth century also tends to obscure other influences on newspaper format. These need careful study, but the existing histories provide some hints. Publishers from different countries copied one another's contents as well as designs. Newspapers in England imitated the formats of continental publishers. American newspapers imported the style of large-format papers from England, even though the stamp and paper taxes had little impact in the United States. Design tastes seem to have been cosmopolitan. The English-speaking press favored Georgian classicism, with its preference for symmetrical arrangement.

In the nineteenth century, the parallel rise of advertising typography and emergence of deck headlines point to other contemporary tastes. The high-contrast, variegated, and frequently embellished Victorian style became common in all forms of commercial and industrial design during the century. The style invaded newspapers slowly, first appearing in Parisian dailies before being imitated in the United States. The technical wizardry of the blanket papers took meaning not so much from the pressures of news and circulation as from the prevailing attitudes. The publisher of the single-issue *Constellation* wrote, "It cannot be excelled in its typographical beauty — in its artistic splendor — in its general imperialism of thought and design" (Hutt 57). Besides reflecting the style of the Victorian era, the blanket newspaper shared an admiration for industry widespread in the era and also embodied the American preoccupation with doing things big.

The influence of changing styles and conventional genres has been largely ignored in part because of the questions driving the received history. By asking who was first—which newspaper introduced particular headlines or other layout elements first—most accounts slid easily into technical developments, disregarding stylistic antecedents as well as contemporaries outside newspapers. Asking who was the biggest concentrated attention on a few newspapers, principally in large cities. Asking which papers survived the longest assured the discovery of a degree of conservatism in newspaper layout. All these factors combine to produce a history of competition, of winners and losers, not of stylistic cooperation and conventional differentiation.

Further study might reveal that newspaper layouts have reflected contemporary culture and elaborated a stylistic code. Design may distinguish urban from rural newspapers and dailies from weeklies. Among large city newspapers, layout (as well as content) may differentiate national from local newspapers. Newspapers may also encode positions along the political spectrum, some papers adopting a conservative dress and others seeking to appear radical. That popular and so-called quality newspapers are different breeds is common knowledge in Britain, just as newspapers "of record" are viewed as distinct from the tabloid press in the United States. Layout—the format, headlines, and make-up of the newspaper page—plays no small role in the newspaper's identity. As styles change in culture, they may also spread into newspapers, amplifying the distinctions within a code of layout.

The Founding of Modernist Layout

The received history of newspaper layout emerged from the modernist ferment immediately before, during, and after the Great War of 1914–18. Movements in art and design upset the central role of representational painting in art. Cubists disintegrated figurative art and began assembling images from typography, clipping and pasting newspaper headlines and text into collages. The newspaper, whatever its informational value, became an image suitable for art because of its very ordinariness. The Dada movement asserted that a whole range of cultural artifacts could be claimed by art, including the lowly toilet bowl, and Bauhaus artists fused artistic form with industrial function. Artists and designers from Europe brought these ideas to the United States, where they had fled to escape the war. Their influence was first felt in advertising and magazine design, as well as in the crafts and architecture (Hurlburt; Meggs).

During and after the war, the tendency to design the entire front page as a visual unit became widespread. The left-to-right pattern of make-up had begun giving way to a concern for the top of the page in the late nineteenth century. The primary position for news moved to the right corner. Banner headlines, used to sensationalize anti-Spanish sentiment in William Randolph Hearst's *New York Journal* in the mid-1890s, carried the eye to the right corner and created right-angle shapes in what came to be called *brace* layout. Banners worked on a much larger scale than their deck predecessors, dominating more of the page. Their dark typography also made areas of body text appear gray (by simultaneous contrast). Stronger headlines and illustrations could enliven the gray mass and help turn the page into a canvas on which visual elements could be designed. Newspapers experimented with symmetrical make-up, balancing items of equal visual weight on either side of the page, and with horizontal make-up, running articles across the entire page. These changes occurred slowly, appearing only to vanish and reappear, but were in full control at many newspapers during and after the war (see Figure 2.5 on p. 40).

The systematic application of modern design to newspapers began in 1916, when the typographer Ben Sherbow was hired to redesign the *New York Tribune*. Sherbow used a stop-

FIGURE 5.5.
Streamlined
layout.
Linotype News
[Brooklyn]
Sept. 1930: 1.
Rpt. in Allen
331.

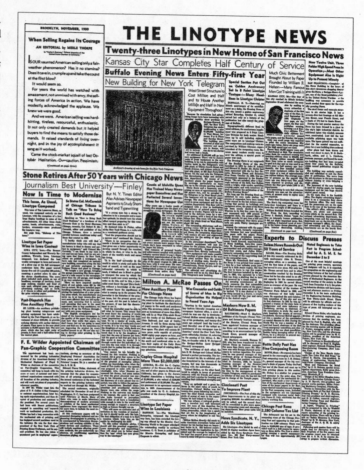

watch to test the readability of headlines and sought to make the newspaper a thing of beauty (Hutt). His principal innovations were to apply a single typeface, Bodoni, in various weights as the newspaper's headline dress and to replace the standard capitals with upper- and lowercase headlines (see Chapter 4). Considered a radical departure for newspapers of the day, Sherbow's design was the typographic expression of progressive-reform thinking. Although the *Tribune* design survived the merger with the *Herald* and continued in the international edition after the combined paper folded, the spread of modern design depended on other reformers.

John Allen, who watched Sherbow's experiments as a young employee of the Mergenthaler Linotype Company, advanced the modern cause not only by redesigning successive issues of the *Linotype News* but also by writing a series of books to expound modern precepts. Allen called his version of Sherbow's reforms *streamlining*, the term that has come to refer to the reigning commercial design style of the 1930s (see Figure 5.5). The modernism Allen founded needs to be described in blunt and dramatic terms to match the polemical ambitions of the movement. Allen proposed no less than a revolution, overturning all that had gone before.

He was joined by the publishers of major dailies in the United States and Britain, who shifted responsibility for page make-up from printers to editors and began hiring typographic consultants. Stanley Morison at the London *Times*, the magazine designer Heyworth Campbell at the New York *Morning Telegraph*, Allen Hutt at the *Daily Worker* in England, advertising typographer Gilbert P. Farrar at the *Los Angeles Times*, and others implemented Allen's prescription for streamlining. Modern newspaper design soon acquired all the trappings of a movement (Hutt). The consultants redesigned dozens of newspapers, and competitions emerged to reward papers that changed, to encourage the doubters, and to provide authoritative sanction and validation for modern design. The first such contest was the Ayer Awards, founded in 1931 by the N. W. Ayer & Son advertising agency of Philadelphia. The Sherbow design of the *Herald Tribune* was an early and frequent winner.

The modernists created from the long and varied history of newspaper design a single villain: traditional layout. The *ancien régime* destined to be overthrown by the modern revolution was described with the most derogatory air: It was born of irrational foreign tax policies and bred of a reactionary conservatism. It was nourished on the degenerate typography of nineteenth-century advertising. It spread a slavish deference to the antique mechanical limits that had long since been overcome. At best, traditional layout was the product of the whims of history, thriving on neglect. The modernists forwarded these views subtly and indirectly, by providing a history that could excoriate tradition with the scalpel of seemingly neutral and objective fact.

The traditional design under attack was in fact the newspaper of the Victorian style. It was tightly packed and chaotic, a window on the disorderly world decorated with the sinewy vines of Art Nouveau origin. In place of that style, modernists proposed a return to many of the typographic traits of the seventeenth-century book-inspired newspapers. Allen and his successors considered the Victorian style too deeply entrenched to be overcome by mere fashion. Style was capricious, and the modernists, themselves following the intellectual fashion of the time, looked for causes outside social custom and human taste. To invoke the influence of fashion would place traditional and modern design on equal footing, rather than establishing the incontrovertible authority of the modern style.

*P*rinciples of Design

The modernists sought to justify their own design notions as an intelligent and permanent response to the dumb chance and superstition of traditional ways. Science and philosophy seemed the surest route to a positive knowledge of correct layout. For the remainder of the twentieth century, practitioners and scholars of journalistic typography turned to several fields of thought: legibility studies and design principles foremost, but also proxemics and architecture. All of these approaches seek to establish final authority through scientific investigation and philosophical axioms. They served three ends: functional, aesthetic, and rhetorical. These purposes, articulated succinctly early in the century (O'Shaughnessy), have been consistently set forth in modernist textbooks and research reports in commonplace terms: "to convey information," "to please the eye," and "to attract attention. "

The science of legibility promised to provide an empirical foundation for typographic decisions (see Chapter 4). Legibility aimed for maximum efficiency by measuring how different designs affected speed, fatigue, and other factors in reading. In line with modern precepts, headlines of mostly lowercase letters were found to be more legible than block capitals, romans more than italics, and serifs more than sans serifs. Flush-left text was found to be more legible than justified (aligned left and right) or centered text. Legibility scientists measured reading by time and motion studies that had parallels in behaviorism and in Taylorism, a movement that followed inventor Frederick W. Taylor's turn-of-the-century prescriptions for efficient industrial production.

⬛ Design principles, the second source for modern ideas, were derived from advertising. Although advertising agencies appeared early

FIGURE 5.6. Principles of design: contrast, balance, rhythm, proportion, unity. Compiled from De Lopatecki 16, 28, 37, 45, 53.

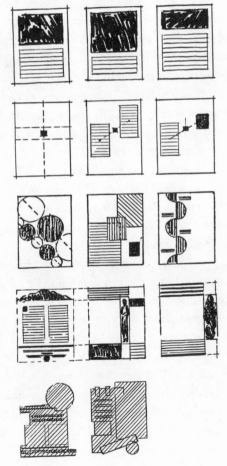

in the nineteenth century, the field did not become widely professionalized, with associations, publications, and ethical codes, until the twentieth. Early textbooks set the pattern of conceptualizing and teaching advertising according to sets of principles, which distilled the collective philosophy of the craft (e.g., Starch). After agencies began providing layout services, experienced "admen" formulated principles for layout (Osborn; Young). The influential textbook *Advertising Theory and Practice*, written by Charles Sandage in 1936, made layout principles a fixture in advertising education for the next half-century.

The most thorough exposition of design principles was forwarded by Eugene De Lopatecki in the 1930s (Figure 5.6). His set of five principles—contrast, balance, proportion, rhythm, and unity—has been adopted with few variations by all subsequent writers. The principles employ the elements and attributes of form within the frame of the page (Dondis). Good contrast emphasizes (usually) one element. Good balance distributes forms equally around focal center (slightly above arithmetic center) according to their weight (darker and larger items being heavier). Good rhythm establishes a sequence (from large to small, dark to light), directing the observer's eye. Good proportion divides up the space without being obvious (in the Western version) or with utter clarity (in the Eastern version). Good unity aligns the forms to create a single silhouette.

De Lopatecki approached layout as a philosophy, proposing a system of first principles that could be reliably employed to guide aesthetic judgments. Although he derived his ideas from the accumulated wisdom of practitioners, he made the principles more authoritative by referring to Greek aesthetics. Advertising and journalism have long been professionally distinct, if not hostile, but newspaper artists and typographers have usually straddled the divide. The principles of design entered journalism through typographers (e.g., O'Shaughnessy) and through graphic design education (Rand; Lauer), eventually becoming a staple in design and editing courses and handbooks. Writers usually echoed De Lopatecki's appeal to Greek philosophy to argue that the principles are time-honored and logical, providing neutral and objective standards for judging layout.

The principles were simply asserted as self-evident and axiomatic (e.g., Moen). They were so often repeated in textbooks and teaching that any sense of their recent origin was lost (e.g., Nelson). One effort to verify their universality by scientific tests found that layouts following the principles were no more pleasing than layouts that deliberately violated them (Martin). Moreover, naïve subjects preferred symmetry to asymmetrical balance and obvious to obscure proportion. The study (presented as a paper to the Association for Education in Journalism in 1964) was never published, and the principles continued to be affirmed as innate, natural to the human sense of beauty.

In fact, design principles are ideological; they impose a modernist standard. Despite the ostensibly neutral terms, each principle acts against the traditional style. Asymmetrical balance is clearly promoted over traditional symmetry, high contrast over low, and so on. Most descriptions and examples provided to illustrate the principles were also partisan celebrations of modernist layout. Open space is preferred to replete, geometric arrangement to biomorphic, simple to decorative, and so forth. The centered, all-capital deck headlines in diverse typefaces and the random and top-heavy make-up with complex, interlocking shapes could not be countenanced under the modernist regime of design principles.

The intolerance among modernists for the traditional style was palpable. They did not like the dense and disorderly newspaper. Their disdain was visceral and moral. Hutt called mixed typography "obscene" (183), and García called the dogleg shapes of brace make-up "sinful" (46). The small scale of headlines and narrow columns edged with column rules were condemned as a dull wilderness compared to the grand scale of modernist style. Design consultants and educators alike employed mercantile metaphors (what Craig calls "promotional ideology" [25]) and gender stereotypes to press for change. The front page was a shop window, its typography a suit of clothes (Allen). Traditional layout was prissy and weak (Arnold). Traditional newspapers were gray ladies, not only bland but presumably feeble. Modern makeovers by contrast were robust, sturdy, and masculine. The traditional-modern divide spilled over into scholarly research (summarized in Barnhurst and Nerone), where traditional newspapers were labeled dull and stubborn resisters of fresh and lively modernism.

Proxemics and the Role of White Space

An important effect of the modernist revolution was to change the conception of space in the newspaper. By the 1950s, many papers had accepted streamlining, and the lower-case, flush-left headlines opened up space on the page. Some newspapers shifted to lighter fonts for headlines and replaced column rules with buffers of white space. In the United States, these changes accompanied the shift to larger body typefaces. The scale of pictures also increased. The open, spacious pages displaying fewer and larger items produced a general effect quite unlike the tight packing that had characterized newspapers for more than two hundred years.

Edmund C. Arnold, who succeeded John Allen as editor of the *Linotype News* and later headed the graphic arts program at Syracuse University, pushed forward the functional modernist project to simplify and clean up the newspaper. He redesigned dozens of newspapers, spoke widely at press seminars, and published several books on newspaper design that became standard reference texts in journalism

> *Journalism— an ability to meet the challenge of filling the space.*
>
> — *Rebecca West*

FIGURE 5.7.
Spatial layout.
Newsday 21
July 1969: 1.
Rpt. in Hutt
208.

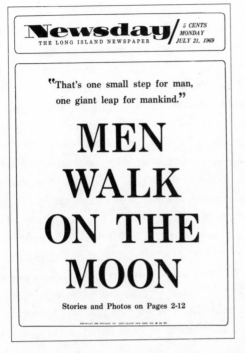

Newsday / 5 CENTS / *MONDAY* / *JULY 21, 1969*

THE LONG ISLAND NEWSPAPER

"That's one small step for man, one giant leap for mankind."

MEN WALK ON THE MOON

Stories and Photos on Pages 2-12

education as well as at newspapers. He was joined by designers such as Clive Irving, best known for his work at the *Observer* of London and his consulting on the trend-setting *Newsday* of Long Island, and by editors such as Harold Evans, who supervised the redesign of the British *Northern Echo*, adding large streamlined headlines and wide spacebands between columns, before moving to the London *Sunday Times* (see Hutt for examples).

These journalists and consultants increased the space and scale of newspaper layout during a period that saw an increased interest in the role of space in culture (see Figure 5.7). During the 1950s and early 1960s, a variety of scholarly studies suggested that a society's attitudes about space are reflected in visual artifacts. This new science, called *proxemics*, came principally from anthropologists, who suggested that space sets the tone for communication and can override what is being said. Edward Hall's books on nonverbal language reached a popular as well as scholarly readership. Their most memorable example demonstrated that people of different cultures do not leave the same space between themselves during conversation. Powerful individuals in hierarchical societies, it was thought, moved in closer. Visual arts and artifacts such as newspaper layouts were considered raw data that could also yield clues to how a society conceived of space, revealing the structure of social relations and power (Fisher). The science of proxemics interpreted the larger interpersonal space in America, for example, as a sign of egalitarianism.

Many other aspects of culture coincided with this celebration of spatiality. Suburbs with expansive lawns and detached houses appeared and burgeoned in the United States. International clothing fashions became open and unadorned. The planet was said to have entered the space age. Under the theory of proxemics, the imprint of these trends—the assertion of a spacious and democratic ideal—can be found in the generous margins and simplified typography of the New York *Herald Tribune*, redesigned in the mid-1960s by Peter Palazzo. Although the newspaper ceased publishing shortly after instituting the changes, Palazzo's pages are still widely admired for capturing the spirit of the times (Evans).

The shift to spacious layout in the 1960s, like so much else in the newspaper, has been attributed to technological change.

FIGURE 5.8. Irregular use of increased space. *Arizona Journal* 11 July 1962: 1. Rpt. in Emery 288.

Newspapers began replacing their mechanical typesetters with photochemical technology. Especially at small newspapers, offset lithography, which prints from flat plates treated chemically, began to supplant raised letterpress printing. The new technology allowed greater freedom than the old, but either method allowed the adding of space. Certainly streamlining

184

was possible without photo-offset production. Some pages produced on the older machinery have so much space that the layouts seem ready to come unglued (Figure 5.8). The new technology may have helped newspaper editors and consultants change the design, but the people, not the machines, set the course of action. Their designs are of a piece with industrial and commercial products of the period.

The concern for white space has become a fixture in newspaper design textbooks (e.g., García; Feinberg and Itule) and has contributed to the understanding of how newspapers communicate. Scholars have suggested that space plays a central role in defining meaning. Walter Ong, whose studies of the effects of technology on literacy first appeared in the 1960s, echoes the common assumption among journalism educators that white space in printing has taken on significance as a pause, the visual equivalent of silence. Newspapers that are tightly filled, he contends, leave no room for argument or dispute. They are a sign of plenitude and closure, suggesting the self-consistency and formality of final authority. Adding space would work to open the form and loosen the grip of visual authority.

The spacious newspaper pages of the 1960s do appear more accessible. The large scale of down-style, lowercase headlines and the generous buffers of space seem youthful and make older layout styles seem impenetrable. But the style had another, unintended ramification. Space and scale were added at the expense of content. The newspaper had to become more choosy about what appeared on the front page. The significance of front-page treatment probably increased as newspapers got fatter and added sections (of which more later), so that many items, in the common phrase, got "buried" inside. Between 1950 and 1970, the number of stories on a typical American front page declined from roughly seventeen to seven (Barnhurst and Nerone). Paradoxically, a sparsely populated front page, more open in form, was less open in content.

Page Architecture and the Grid

Modernist designers did not ignore the effects of depopulating the front page and multiplying the interior pages and sections. To compensate for these changes, they turned to organizational ideas from the emerging field of graphic design. Courses in commercial art and advertising layout appeared early in the twentieth century and by the 1950s had expanded and become institutionalized as academic departments (with corresponding textbooks, e.g., Scott). The faculty of art colleges in Switzerland trained a generation of graphic designers to work in a precisely ordered and mathematical style that made its way to the United States in the 1960s. The resulting International typographical style paralleled its namesake movement in architecture (Meggs).

Like other forms of modern design, the Swiss school was rooted in abstract art movements of the early twentieth century. The Bauhaus abjured the decorative role of design in the Victorian era and proposed a new role: design that reflects the internal structure and clarifies the function of commercial and

FIGURE 5.9. Truly modular grid. Massimo Vignelli design for the *Herald* [New York] 8 Apr. 1971: 1. Rpt. in Hurlburt 36.

industrial products. Buildings in the International Style had clean and open façades and a rational interior organization built on standardized units or modules. The typographical version of the style arranged layouts on an underlying grid, a mathematically proportioned latticework of horizontal and vertical lines and spaces (Figure 5.9). The grid was most widely adopted where space was most generous, in magazines such as *Look* under Alan Hurlburt and in large-scale posters.

Swiss style reached newspapers in the 1970s. The *Minneapolis Tribune* unveiled its new design built on a grid in 1971 (Figure 5.10). The British artist Frank Ariss, who directed the project, called the grid a piece of graphics engineering (Hutt). Newspapers had always divided pages into columns, but some stories were laid out in column widths unrelated to other columns on the page, on what was called a *bastard* measure. The Ariss grid used different column widths, but they had proportional, not bastard, measures (Wallace). Grids applied the same control to vertical organization. The system worked like a modernist window shade. Ordinary shades move up and down to any height, but modern architects installed shades that had only three or four positions, determined by the mathematical proportions of a grid.

Such window shades seem particularly limiting, but they reflect an ancient notion that beauty can be mathematically derived. The proportions of the Acropolis and the Parthenon inspired Renaissance writers and artists to define beauty as the geometric space surrounding the human form. Claude Bragdon reintroduced the notion in 1910, along with other art teachers of the period, but the architect Le Corbusier worked out the most elaborate and influential application in his *Modulor*. Architects justify the grid on the grounds not only of beauty but also of industrial necessity. Building materials can be most efficiently manufactured for construction if they have regular proportions, both height and width. A modular system limits variety but can make many small, prefabricated parts fit together to build a large edifice.

The Ariss grid limited, but only somewhat, the freedom to begin and end pictures and stories anywhere on the page. Other designs of the period were more exacting. Massimo Vignelli's grid for the *Herald*, a short-lived New York Sunday newspaper (see Figure 5.9), divided the page into six vertical (columns) and seventeen horizontal units (Hurlburt). The resulting layouts are truly modular, because each piece of text and each image has a proportional two-dimensional relation-

FIGURE 5.11. Summary front page. *Left, New York Herald Tribune* 3 Mar. 1937: 1; *right, Gist* experimental page from same day's content. From Brucker 99–100.

ship with everything else on the page. These proportional relations were at the core of Swiss design. Most newspapers that copied the style ignored the limits on bastard measures and the controls on vertical proportions. In newspapers, the style became strongly connected with a preference for horizontal make-up, which was never central to the Swiss school. What journalists called "modular" layout merely put every story into a rectangle, usually horizontal, a discipline at once less rigorous and more confining than envisioned in the International typographic style.

At least some control was considered a necessary response to the increase of space on the page. Newspapers of the 1960s had gotten so loose as to seem anarchic. The grid allowed a great deal of that space to remain, but under disciplined conditions. Ariss, in fact, increased space further by leaving a full blank line between every paragraph of body text and allowing space to remain at the end of stories that ran short. The influence of Swiss style on newspapers has generally been credited with producing a clean, uncluttered, and organized look.

The modernist penchant for orderliness and structure became pronounced in newspapers of the 1970s. Indexes and summaries of inside stories had appeared with the earliest modern redesigns. A front page filled completely with summaries and indexes was first proposed in the 1930s with the hypothetical newspaper *Gist* (Brucker; see Figure 5.11). For the next forty years, these elements grew more prominent and occupied more space on real front pages, absorbing

FIGURE 5.12. Decorated feature page. *Washington Star* 3 Oct. 1979. From García 16.

greater editorial time and attention. Indexes served the dual role of mapping not only the contents of the paper but also its physical arrangement. The structure of the newspaper reflected the organization of newspaper reporting, divided between news and features and subdivided into increasingly narrow specialties. The division of the physical newspaper into sections and special pages established a hierarchy clearly charted by indexes (Ong).

As the Swiss style took over the general organization of the newspaper, other movements in graphic design affected the typography, illustration, and layout of the feature pages. Two styles, descended from the eclectic collages of Cubism and inspired by expressionism and surrealism, came to the fore of general graphic design: the New York school in the 1950s and the Push Pin studio in the 1960s (Meggs). At newspapers beginning in the 1970s, feature pages were invaded by decorative typography and experimental illustrations. Some pages were taken over by a single design. These poster layouts broke out of the constraints not only of typography but also of news (Figure 5.12). They fused art and the practical newspaper—a modernist achievement that resurrected the showy full-page layouts of the mid–nineteenth century.

The influence of graphic design on newspapers during the 1970s brought the modernist style to its culmination. The Society of Newspaper Design, formed in 1979, began to publish annuals that institutionalized modernism. The small size of reproductions in these books rewarded only those designs that stood out when greatly reduced or seen from more than an arm's length. The newspaper as a form had become the object of aesthetic contemplation, fully colonized by modern design. The big, roomy designs of the United States were imitated widely, and consultants carried the tenets of modern thinking into newspapers in developing countries. The design style seemed securely backed by the sciences of legibility and proxemics, by the philosophy of design principles, and by the mathematics of modular layout and the grid. Recent designs have reacted against these ideas, but many newspapers remain in the modernist mold. They deserve scrutiny before we turn to later developments.

Seeing the Newspaper

*T*he newspaper you usually read is probably controlled by modernist concepts. This exercise requires that you distance yourself from your habits of reading and come at the newspaper with fresh eyes. Your first goal is to become aware of the stylistic quality of the newspaper and to identify the period of design it follows. You will also try to identify what attitudes and values the newspaper reinforces through layout and design. All you will need is a copy or two of the newspaper, a ruler, and some colored pencils or crayons.

Begin by studying the stylistic qualities of the newspaper. List the characteristics of headlines. Are they set in uniform or diverse typefaces? Do they have serifs? Are they in all capitals, italics, or upper- and lowercase romans? How extreme is the range between the largest and the smallest? Are they centered or laid out flush left? Next list the characteristics of space. Are the columns divided by ruled lines or by spaces? Do the spaces appear thick or thin? Notice the width of indentations and the spaces between paragraphs. Are there any areas of unfilled space elsewhere on the page? Now examine the underlying structure or grid. Are the columns narrow or wide? If they vary, measure them to see if their width has a proportional relationship (1:2, 2:3, or the like). Do they start and stop at proportional vertical intervals (like modernist window shades)? Study the overall design of the sections. Are all pages identical typographically? Does the front page differ? Do you find posterlike pages in some sections?

From this cursory examination, you should be able to categorize the newspaper roughly by style. Unless the newspaper follows the Swiss style dogmatically, you will probably find some variation between sections. Sometimes the front page is the slowest to change, carrying forward at least a few design characteristics of an earlier style. Designers of the Swiss school condemn such differences. Others categorically label anything but the latest style bad, old-fashioned, and dated. Period references in the newspaper continue to invoke the predominant values of an earlier time, which may or may not be desirable.

Even the most visually conservative newspapers do not withstand the forces of change in fashion. Although some front pages retain the flavor of another era, they also organize space and index contents according to modernist rules. The differences are a matter of degree. Instead of making a categorical distinction, you will probably have to hedge your label for the newspaper. It may have a front page with the scale and space of the 1960s and the organization and indexing of Swiss design, but use mixed typography from an earlier period. Some inside sections may be firmly working in the tradition of conceptual poster pages. The occasional newspaper retains turn-of-the-century typography and make-up on its editorial page.

Having carefully observed the stylistic qualities of the paper, stop to consider your reactions to them. What don't you like about the typography, the use of space, or the organization? What seems particularly appealing to you? Try to translate those personal reactions into broader judgments. Ask people you know from your social, political, or ethnic group if they share your opinions. What changes would they make? Finally, speculate about how people from other groups might react to the newspaper's style. Would changes in the style affect them adversely?

Those speculations lead to the second phase of the exercise, which requires that you examine the newspaper to discover the attitudes and values it reinforces through layout and design. List the various groups that live in the area where the newspaper circulates. These might include not only racial, religious, and ethnic groups but also people of distinct gender, age, physical ability, and sexual orientation. List the types of workers and also any interest groups based on avocation. Once the list is complete, cross off any groups to which you belong. Create a key by assigning a color to each of the groups remaining. If you don't have enough pencils, supplement the colors with symbols (stars, check marks, etc.) or letters and numbers.

With your color key in hand, read the entire issue of the newspaper, carefully skimming every item and circling or coloring in each reference to any group on your list with the assigned color. If you discover groups missing from your list, add them to the key. Be sure to mark or color each item dark enough to stand out. Code not only the text but also the drawings, logos, and photographs in advertisements as well as in news and features. Also note whether the content places the group in a positive light. When you have coded the entire paper, make notes that summarize what you found. Besides the obvious measures of how often groups appeared or how extensive their coverage, note the placement of stories by group. Were they on the section fronts, the tops of pages? What sorts of stories were juxtaposed with them? What patterns apply to coverage of minorities in general? How many groups were completely absent?

The Politics of Layout

Design puts art in the service of communication. Through much of art history, artists worked for patrons, whom they had to please, but artists since the Romantic period have been seen as autonomous, serving only their muse. Newspaper designers and layout editors need to serve more than themselves or such abstractions as art and news. They can serve readers from many groups, not only the majority but also minorities who may or may not read the newspaper. The surest way to exclude readers, and to discourage nonreaders

FIGURE 5.13. Horizontal "modular" layout of the 1970s reaches into Latin America. *El Comercio* [Lima, Peru] 30 July 1989: 1.

from becoming readers, is to ignore them.

◙ Newspaper style, even though it changes with fashions, tends to cater to specific tastes. This can be most clearly seen in the developing world, where newspapers are often designed by consultants from industrialized countries. In Peru, a country racked by political violence in the 1980s, the oldest and most powerful newspaper (Figure 5.13) bore a design patterned after the international typographical style, serene and sedate amid the tumult, with horizontal rectangular stories (Barnhurst, "Layout"). A design imported from the peaceful Swiss cantons, via the tranquil United States of the 1970s, served primarily the educated of the professional and commercial classes. The layout clearly projects an image insulated from the ravages of the economic collapse, drug violence, and guerrilla wars.

The make-up of the newspaper also serves particular interests. In Peru, the insurgency claimed to be driven by race, pitting the native *campesino* against the Europeanized city dweller (Barnhurst, "Terrorism"). The newspaper's official policy was to place the insurgents off the front page. In the United States, the front page can likewise be a racial, sexual, and social preserve. In your examination of the newspaper, your most telling discovery was probably the lack of coverage of minorities. If you live in a city with a large, diverse population, minority stories are often negative and placed low in the hierarchy of make-up, unless minority people and events seem threatening. Young people, who must be attracted as readers if newspapers are to survive, are notably absent from the front page. Newspapers ignore many other groups as well.

The organization of stories, which is usually proposed as a convenience to readers, also conveys judgments. Scholars have recently argued that television takes on meanings from juxtaposition, such as an ad for a pregnancy test that unintentionally interrupts a story about childlessness (Caputi; Berger). A similar pattern occurs as a result of the modernist organizational schemes in newspapers. In Peru, official policy at several newspapers places coverage of the insurgency on the police page, surrounded by common criminals. Activists have objected to similar groupings that create guilt by association, such as the placement of AIDS medical stories next to gay rights activities or incidents of child molestation (Roshan). The coupling of violent crime with civil rights in newspaper layout has appeared in the coverage of women and African Americans, as well as lesbians and gay men. Packaging the news in many cases serves the editor's stereotypes rather than the reader's convenience or interests.

> *R*eading someone else's newspaper is like sleeping with someone else's wife. Nothing seems to be precisely in the right place.
>
> — *Malcolm Bradbury*

Layout is an act of empathy, requiring a designer to consider readers, some of whom may not be liked or respected. Integrated layout requires not color, gender, and age blindness and the like, but thoughtful attention to those divisions. A few years ago, a high-school journalist in an Ohio community with a growing minority population was quoted as saying, "We've got too many white people on this page. You can't have a page with no black people" (Wilkerson). Creating pages free of prejudice may also demand at least some freedom from modernist dogma. Smaller headlines and less space may serve a greater good than beauty. Planned disorder may be the only way to integrate content. Some of the positive confidence in scientific studies and philosophical laws might be profitably surrendered to deference, sensitivity, and good manners. Beauty resides there, too.

*P*ostmodernism and the Future

In the 1980s, the postmodern style invaded graphic design from its origins in art and architecture. Postmodernism ransacks history, combining disparate stylistic effects with a mix of nostalgia and irony. It is a conservative movement that concentrates on illusion and surface effects. *USA Today*, which began publishing in 1982, incorporates the devices of Victorian newspapers, including narrow columns, varied headlines, vertical makeup, column rules, and a smaller scale overall. These are employed not in the mode of Victorian content but ironically for short snippets of text with amusing graphics and many pictures, in the mode of fast food, sound bites, and rock videos. Although other newspapers anticipated its use of graphics and color, *USA Today* has become a bellwether, marking the beginning of a new stylistic period (Barnhurst and Ellis).

> *A* headline is not an act of journalism, it is an act of marketing.
>
> — *Harold Evans*

🌀 Multiplying the number of smaller elements on the front page might allow more diversity, but the design does not of itself produce that result. The front pages of *USA Today* are no more integrated than were Victorian front pages. No style is necessarily wedded to a particular type of coverage. Instead, newspapers follow a style to invoke iconic meanings.

One meaning is power and authority. The visual appearance of the *Times* of London and the *New York Times* has become a sign of the prestige and power of those newspapers. Their conservatism springs in part from a reluctance to dilute their authority visually by changing design. Many community and minority newspapers aspire to imitate elite design, as a sign of their own serious purpose and professional mastery. In reaction to that approach, some newspapers of the U.S. feminist press have adopted a homemade design, with typewriter text and rub-on headlines that both sustain and confront women's traditional tasks in business and in the home (Figure 5.14).

Another meaning is populism and currency. Newspapers in the 1980s imitated the layout of *USA Today* as a sign of being up-to-date. The periodic shifts in design style allow newspapers to reassert their commitment to timeliness and their ability to keep up with the world. By reflecting current fashion, newspapers also suggest their responsiveness to popular tastes. The visual appearance of *USA Today* opposes the

FIGURE 5.14.
Homemade and clerical effects in an alternative women's newspaper. *Exponent II* [Boston] 7:3 (Spring 1981): 1, 7.

FIGURE 5.15.
Postmodern
magazine
pages. Two
spreads with
digital-
geometric
type, *Emigre
#19*. Rpt. in
*Communication
Arts* 34.1
(Mar./Apr.
1992): 67.

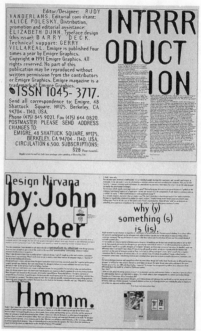

authoritarian posture of other elite newspapers, whether its democratic posture is mere illusion or substance. Only the rare newspaper rejects elite fashion. The layout of some Native American newspapers honors the styles of their own culture, in defiance of the elite press (Ganje). But for the most part, designers are trapped by their own stereotypes (Moriarty and Rohe).

Designers such as Robert Lockwood, who generally work in the modernist mode, also flirt with the historicism and irony of postmodernism. His redesign of the *Los Angeles Herald*, for example, refers to the constructivist art of the 1920s, opposing the "slick corporate designs" with a "rough-edged vitality" in the service of conservative corporate interests (64). Yet newspaper design has not self-consciously embraced postmodernism, as some magazines have done (Figure 5.15).

Asked to foretell the future of newspaper design, members of an American Press Institute seminar in 1988 had two types of predictions. One anticipated more indexes, more grids, more space. The other foresaw more fax, more barcode, more database. In sum, the state of ideas in the field seemed to offer only more of the same, more looking back to modernism and/or more looking forward to new technology. A critical sense of the role of design in culture must await some future movement.

WORKS CITED

PREFACE

Ferguson, Eugene S. *Engineering and the Mind's Eye*. Cambridge: MIT P, 1992.

Fidler, Roger. "Mediamorphosis, or the Transformation of Newspapers into a New Medium." *Media Studies Journal* 4.4 (1991): 115–25.

CHAPTER 1
SEEING THE NEWSPAPER

Barnhurst, Kevin G. "Analyzing Images: Visual Communication Theory and the Newspaper." Unpublished manuscript, 1992.

Barnhurst, Kevin G., and John C. Nerone. "Design Trends in U.S. Front Pages, 1885–1985." *Journalism Quarterly* 68 (1992): 796–804.

Barnhurst, Kevin G., and Ellen Wartella. "Newspapers and Citizenship: Young Adults' Subjective Experience of Newspapers." Critical Studies in Mass Communication 8 (1991): 195–209.

Barthes, Roland. *Mythologies*. New York: Hill, 1972.

"Doll Breaks Drop: Salt Lake Baby Injured in 2-Story Fall." *Salt Lake Telegram* 30 Aug. 1948: 1.

"Fall Injury Fatal to Mother, Autopsy Shows." *Deseret News and Salt Lake Telegram* 14 June 1961: 1.

Ferguson, Eugene S. *Engineering and the Mind's Eye*. Cambridge: MIT P, 1992.

Fidler, Roger. "Mediamorphosis, or the Transformation of Newspapers into a New Medium." *Media Studies Journal* 4.4 (1991): 115–25.

García, Mario R. *Contemporary Newspaper Design*. Englewood Cliffs: Prentice, 1981.

García, Mario R., and Pegie Stark. *Eyes on the News*. St. Petersburg: Poynter, 1991.

Kruger, Barbara. *We Won't Play Nature to Your Culture*. London: Institute of Contemporary Arts, 1983.

Middlestadt, Susan E. "The Effect of Vertical vs. Horizontal Newspaper Article Layout on Perception of the Content of the Article." Unpublished manuscript, 1988.

Rosenblatt, Roger. "Journalism and the Larger Truth." *Time* 2 July 1984: 88.

Varnedoe, Kirk, and Adam Gopnik. *High & Low: Modern Art & Popular Culture*. New York: MoMA, 1990.

CHAPTER 2
UNDERSTANDING PHOTOGRAPHY

Baker, Robert L. "Portraits of a Public Suicide: Photo Treatment by Selected Pennsylvania Dailies." *Newspaper Research Journal* 9.3 (1988): 13–23.

Barnhurst, Kevin G. "The Alternative Vision: Lewis Hine's *Men at Work* in the Dominant Culture." *Photo-Textualities: Reading Photographs and Literary Texts*. Ed. Marsha Bryant. Unpublished manuscript, 1992.

Barthes, Roland. *A Barthes Reader*. Ed. Susan Sontag. New York: Hill, 1982.

Bayer, Jonathan. *Reading Photographs: Understanding the Aesthetics of Photography*. New York: Pantheon, 1977.

Baynes, Ken, ed. *Scoop, Scandal, and Strife: A Study of Photography in Newspapers*. London: Lund, 1971.

Becker, Howard. "Do Photographs Tell the Truth?" *AfterImage* 1 (1978): 9–13.

Benjamin, Walter. "The Work of Art in the Age of Mechanical Reproduction." *Illuminations*. Ed. Hannah Arendt. New York: Schocken, 1986. 217–51.

Berger, John. *Ways of Seeing*. London: BBC and Penguin, 1972.

Bergin, David P. *Photo Journalism Manual*. Hastings-on-Hudson: Morgan, 1967.

The Best of Photojournalism (annual). New York: Newsweek, 1976.

Bethune, Beverly M. "A Profile of Photojournalists on Two Metropolitan Newspapers." *Journalism Quarterly* 58 (1981): 106–8.

Bolton, Richard, ed. *The Contest of Meaning: Critical Histories of Photography*. Cambridge: MIT P, 1989.

Braive, Michel F. *The Photograph: A Social History*. Trans. David Britt. New York: McGraw, 1966.

Brecheen-Kirkton, Kent. "Visual Silences: How Photojournalism Covers Reality with the Facts." *American Journalism* Winter 1991: 27–34.

Burnett, David. "Freeze Frame: Why Still Pictures Are the Images That Endure." *Dateline* 7 May 1990: 44–48.

Capa, Robert. *Robert Capa Photographs.* Ed. Cornell Capa and Richard Whelan. New York: Knopf, 1985.

Cartier-Bresson, Henri. *The Decisive Moment.* New York: Simon, 1952.

Coke, Van Deren. *The Painter and the Photograph from Delacroix to Warhol.* 1964. Albuquerque: U of New Mexico P, 1972.

Crary, Jonathan. *Techniques of the Observer: On Vision and Modernity in the Nineteenth Century.* October. Cambridge: MIT P, 1990.

Eder, Josef M. *History of Photography.* Trans. Edward Epstean. New York: Columbia UP, 1945.

Edom, Clifton C. *Photojournalism: Principles and Practices.* Dubuque: Brown, 1976.

Eisenstaedt, Alfred. *Eisenstaedt Remembers.* Ed. Doris C. O'Neil. Boston: Little, 1990.

Evans, Harold. *Eyewitness: Twenty-Five Years through World Press Photos.* London: Quiller, 1981.

———. *Pictures on a Page.* New York: Holt, 1978.

Ezickson, Aaron J. *Get That Picture! The Story of the News Cameraman.* New York: National Library, 1938.

Faber, John. *Great News Photos and the Stories behind Them.* 1960. New York: Dover, 1978.

Fedler, Fred, Tim Counts, and Paul Hightower. "Changes in Wording of Cutlines Fail to Reduce Photographs' Offensiveness." *Journalism Quarterly* 59 (1982): 633–37.

Fellig, Arthur. *Weegee.* Ed. Louis Stettner. New York: Knopf, 1977.

Fishman, Mark. *Manufacturing the News.* Austin: U of Texas P, 1980.

Foucault, Michel. *The Order of Things: An Archaeology of the Human Sciences.* New York: Vintage, 1973.

Fox, Rodney, and Robert Kerns. *Creative News Photography.* Ames: Iowa State UP, 1961.

Freund, Gisele. *Photography and Society.* Boston: Godine, 1980.

Fulton, Marianne, ed. *Eyes of Time: Photojournalism in America.* Boston: Bulfinch, 1989.

Galassi, Peter. *Before Photography: Painting and the Invention of Photography.* New York: MoMA, 1981.

Gans, Herbert. *Deciding What's News.* New York: Vintage, 1979.

Geraci, Philip C. *Photojournalism: Making Pictures for Publication.* Dubuque: Kendall, 1973.

Gernsheim, Helmut, and Alison Gernsheim. *The History of Photography.* 1955. New York: McGraw, 1969.

Gibson, James J. *The Perception of the Visual World.* Cambridge: Riverside-Houghton, 1950.

Gidal, Tim N. *Modern Photojournalism: Origin and Evolution, 1910–1933.* Trans. Maureen Oberli-Turner. New York: Macmillan, 1973.

Gitlin, Todd. *The Whole World Is Watching: Mass Media in the Making and Unmaking of the New Left.* Berkeley: U of California P, 1980.

Gombrich, E. H. *Art and Illusion: A Study in the Psychology of Pictorial Representation.* 1960. Bollingen Ser. 35, no. 5. Princeton: Princeton UP, 1969.

Goodman, Nelson. *Languages of Art: An Approach to a Theory of Symbols.* 1969. Indianapolis: Hackett, 1976.

Green, Jonathan. *American Photography: A Critical History, 1945 to the Present.* New York: Abrams, 1984.

Griffin, Michael. "Turning to a History of Picture Use: Ekphrasis and Conventions of Picture Description." Unpublished paper, 1986.

Guimond, James, ed. *American Photography and the American Dream.* Chapel Hill: U of North Carolina P, 1991.

Hall, Stuart. "The Determination of News Photographs." *The Manufacture of News: Social Problems, Deviance, and the Mass Media.* Ed. Stanley Cohen and Jock Young. London: Constable, 1981. 226–43.

Hardin, C. L. *Color for Philosophers: Unweaving the Rainbow.* Indianapolis: Hackett, 1989.

Hardt, Hanno. "Words and Images in the Age of Technology." *Media Development* 38.4 (1991): 3–5.

Hauser, Arnold. *The Philosophy of Art History.* New York: Knopf, 1959.

Henderson, Lisa. "Access and Consent in Public Photography." *Image Ethics.* Ed. Larry Gross, John Stuart Katz, and Jay Ruby. New York: Oxford, 1988. 91–107.

Hicks, Wilson. *Words and Pictures: An Introduction to Photojournalism.* New York: Harper, 1952.

Hoy, Frank P. *Photojournalism: The Visual Approach.* Englewood Cliffs: Prentice, 1986.

Hunter, Jefferson. *Image and Word: The Interaction of Twentieth-Century Photographs and Texts.* Cambridge: Harvard UP, 1987.

Hurley, Gerald D., and Angus McDougall. *Visual Impact in Print.* Chicago: Visual Impact, 1971.

Images of Our Times: Sixty Years of Photography from the Los Angeles Times. New York: Abrams, 1987.

Ivins, William M., Jr. *Prints and Visual Communication.* Graphic Art 10. New York: Da Capo, 1969.

Jensen, Robert. "Fighting Objectivity: The Illusion of Journalistic Neutrality in Coverage of the Persian Gulf War." *Journal of Communication Inquiry* 16.1 (1992): 20–32.

Kee, Robert. *The Picture Post Album.* London: Barrie, 1989.

Kerns, Robert L. *Photojournalism: Photography with a Purpose.* Englewood Cliffs: Prentice, 1980.

Kinkaid, James C. *Press Photography*. Cleveland: Am. Photographic, 1936.

Kobre, Kenneth. *Photojournalism: The Professionals' Approach*. Somerville: Curtin, 1980.

Lacayo, Richard, and George Russell. *Eyewitness: One Hundred Fifty Years of Photojournalism*. New York: Oxmore, 1990.

Leekley, Sheryle, and John Leekley. *Moments: The Pulitzer Prize Photographs*. New York: Crown, 1982.

Lester, Paul. *Photojournalism: An Ethical Approach*. Hillsdale: Erlbaum, 1991.

Lester, Paul M., and Ron Smith. "African-American Photo Coverage in *Life, Newsweek* and *Time*, 1937–88." *Journalism Quarterly* 67 (1990): 128–36.

MacDougall, Curtis D. *News Pictures Fit to Print . . . or Are They?* Stillwater: Journalistic Services, 1971.

Manchester, William. *In Our Time: The World as Seen by Magnum Photographers*. New York: Norton, 1989.

Marr, David. *Vision: A Computational Investigation into the Human Representation and Processing of Visual Information*. San Francisco: Freeman, 1982.

McDougall, Angus, and Veita Jo Hampton. *Picture Editing and Layout: A Guide to Better Visual Communication*. Columbia: Vision P, 1990.

McLuhan, Marshall. *Understanding Media, the Extensions of Man*. New York: McGraw, 1964.

Messaris, Paul. "Perceptual Bases of Visual Literacy." Unpublished paper, 1992.

Mitchell, William J. *The Reconfigured Eye: Visual Truth in the Post-Photographic Era*. Cambridge: MIT P, 1992.

Mukerji, Chandra. *From Graven Images: Patterns of Modern Materialism*. New York: Columbia UP, 1983.

Newhall, Beaumont. "The Daguerreotype and the Painter." *Magazine of Art* 42.7 (1949): 249–51.

———. *The History of Photography, 1839 to the Present Day*. New York: MoMA, 1982.

———. *Photography: A Short Critical History*. New York: MoMA, 1938.

Norback, Craig T., and Melvin Gray, eds. *The World's Great News Photos, 1840–1980*. New York: Crown, 1980.

Novitz, David. *Pictures and Their Use in Communication*. The Hague: Nijhoff, 1977.

Orvell, Miles. *The Real Thing: Imitation and Authenticity in American Culture, 1880–1940*. Chapel Hill: U of North Carolina P, 1989.

Panofsky, Erwin. *Meaning in the Visual Arts*. New York: Doubleday, 1955.

———. *Perspective as Symbolic Form*. Trans. Christopher S. Wood.

New York: Zone, 1991.

Phelan, John M. "Image Industry Erodes Political Space." *Media Development* 38.4 (1991): 6–8.

Photojournalism Ethics [special issue]. *Journal of Mass Media Ethics* 2.2 (1987).

Pouncey, Truman. *Photographic Journalism*. Dubuque: Brown, 1946.

Price, Jack. *News Photography*. New York: Industries, 1932.

Rhode, Robert B., and Floyd H. McCall. *Press Photography: Reporting with a Camera*. New York: Macmillan, 1961.

Rosenblum, Barbara. *Photographers at Work: A Sociology of Photographic Styles*. New York: Holmes, 1978.

Rothstein, Arthur. *Photojournalism: Pictures for Magazines and Newspapers*. New York: Am. Photographic, 1956.

Schloss, Carol. *In Visible Light: Photography and the American Writer, 1840–1940*. New York: Oxford, 1987.

Schuneman, R. Smith, ed. *Photographic Communication: Principles, Problems, and Challenges of Photojournalism*. New York: Hastings, 1972.

Schwartz, Dona B. "To Tell the Truth: Codes of Objectivity in Photojournalism." *Communication* 13. 2 (1992): 95–109.

Schwartz, Dona B., and Michael Griffin. "Amateur Photography: The Organizational Maintenance of an Aesthetic Code." *Natural Audiences: Qualitative Research of Media Uses and Effects*. Ed. Thomas R. Lindlof. New York: Ablex, 1987. 198–224.

Schwarz, Heinrich. *Art and Photography: Forerunners and Influences, Selected Essays*. Rochester: Visual Studies Workshop, 1985.

Sekula, Allan. *Photography against the Grain: Essays and Photo Works, 1973–1983*. Halifax: P of the Nova Scotia College of Art and Design, 1984.

———. "War without Bodies." *ArtForum* Nov. 1991: 107–10.

Snyder, Joel. "Picturing Vision." *The Language of Images*. Ed. W. J. T. Mitchell. Chicago: U of Chicago P, 1980. 219–46.

Sontag, Susan. *On Photography*. New York: Farrar, 1973.

Spencer, Otha C. *The Art and Techniques of Journalistic Photography*. Wolfe City: Hennington, 1966.

Steichen, Edward. *The Family of Man*. New York: Simon, 1955.

Stenger, Erich. *The History of Photography*. Trans. Edward Epstean. Easton: Mack, 1939.

Szarkowski, John. *The Photographer's Eye*. New York: MoMA, 1966.

———, ed. *From the Picture Press*. New York: MoMA, 1973.

Taft, Robert. *Photography and the American Scene: A Social History, 1839–1889*. 1938. New York: Dover, 1964.

Thompson, Patricia. "All Faces Are Seen, but Few Are Given Voice: Canonic Generality in Designed Images." *Journal of*

Communication Inquiry 16.2 (1992): 102–17.

Trachtenberg, Alan. *Reading American Photographs: Images as History, Mathew Brady to Walker Evans.* New York: Hill, 1990.

Tuchman, Gaye. *Making News: A Study of the Construction of Reality.* New York: Free, 1980.

Vitray, Laura, John Mills, Jr., and Roscoe Ellard. *Pictorial Journalism.* New York: McGraw, 1939.

Wanta, Wayne. "The Effects of Dominant Photographs: An Agenda-Setting Experiment." *Journalism Quarterly* 65 (1988): 107–11.

Whiting, John R. *Photography Is a Language.* Chicago: Ziff, 1946.

Williams, Raymond. *The Long Revolution.* New York: Columbia UP, 1961.

Worth, Sol. *Studying Visual Communication.* Ed. Larry Gross. Philadelphia: U of Pennsylvania P, 1981.

❆

CHAPTER 3
CRITIQUING CHARTS

Alonzo, William. *The Politics of Numbers.* New York: Russell Sage, 1989.

Arkin, Herbert, and Raymond R. Colton. *Graphs: How to Make and Use Them.* New York: Harper, 1940.

Armytage, W. H. G. *A Social History of Engineering.* Boulder: Westview, 1976.

Berthon, Simon, and Andrew Robinson. *The Shape of the World.* Chicago: Rand, 1990.

Bertin, Jacques. *Semiology of Graphics: Diagrams, Networks, Maps.* Madison: U of Wisconsin P, 1983.

Chatfield, Michael. *A History of Accounting Thought.* Huntington: Krieger, 1977.

Cleveland, W. S. *The Elements of Graphing Data.* Monterey: Wadsworth, 1985.

Cohen, Patricia Cline. *A Calculating People: The Spread of Numeracy in America.* Chicago: U of Chicago P, 1983.

Collins, Rebecca L., et al. "The Vividness Effect: Elusive or Illusory?" *Journal of Experimental Social Psychology* 24 (1988): 1–18.

Combs, Jacqueline A. "*Chicago Tribune* Was Doing Informational Graphics Sixty Years Ago." *Visual Communication Newsletter* Jan. 1991: 4.

Crone, G. R. *Maps and Their Makers.* 5th ed. Folkestone: Dawson, 1978.

Culbertson, H. M., and R. D. Powers. "A Study of Graph

Comprehension Difficulties." *Audio-Visual Communication Review* 7 (1959): 97–100.

Cvengros, Stephen. "A New Force in the Newsroom." *Design: Journal of the Society of Newspaper Design* no. 29 (1988): 35.

David, Prabu. "Accuracy of Visual Perception of Quantitative Graphics: An Exploratory Study." *Journalism Quarterly* 69 (1992): 273–92.

DeParle, Jason. "Painted by Numbers, 1980s Are Rosy to GOP, While Democrats See Red." *New York Times* 26 Sept. 1991, late ed.: B10.

Egan, Timothy. "Oregon Literacy Test Shows Many Lag in Basics." *New York Times* 24 Apr. 1991, late ed.: B7.

"Executive Summary." [Summary of *An Evaluation of Dietary Guidance Graphic Alternatives.*] Cambridge: Bell Associates, 1992.

Ferguson, Eugene S. *Engineering and the Mind's Eye.* Cambridge: MIT P, 1992.

Funkhouser, H. G. "Historical Development of the Graphical Representation of Statistical Data." *Osiris* 3 (1937): 269–404.

Giesecke, Frederick E., et al. *Engineering Graphics.* 2nd ed. New York: Macmillan, 1975.

Gregory, Malcolm S. *History and Development of Engineering.* London: Longman, 1971.

Hallin, Daniel C. "Cartography, Community, and the Cold War." *Reading the News.* Ed. Robert Karl Manoff and Michael Schudson. New York: Pantheon, 1986, 109–45.

———. *The "Uncensored War": The Media and Vietnam.* New York: Oxford, 1986.

Harley, J. B. "Deconstructing the Map." *Cartographica* 26.2 (1989): 1–20.

Have, O. ten. *The History of Accountancy.* Palo Alto: Bay, 1976.

Herbst, Susan. *Numbered Voices.* Chicago: U of Chicago P, 1993.

Hill, Donald. *A History of Engineering in Classical and Medieval Times.* London: Croom, 1984.

Hilliard, Robert D. "The Graphics Explosion: Questions Remain about Roles." *Journalism Quarterly* 66 (1989): 192–94.

History of Cartography. Slide program. Comp. George Kish. Ann Arbor: n.d. 220 slides.

Hollander, Barry A. "Information Graphics and the Bandwagon Effect: Does the Visual Display of Opinion Aid in Persuasion?" Unpublished paper, 1992.

Holmes, Nigel. *Designer's Guide to Creating Charts and Diagrams.* New York: Watson, 1984.

———. *Pictorial Maps.* New York: Watson, 1991.

Huff, Darrell. *How to Lie with Statistics.* New York: Norton, 1954. *Journal of Graphic Design* 6:2 (1988).

Kirby, R. S., et al. *Engineering in History*. New York: McGraw, 1956.

Kosslyn, Stephen M. "Understanding Charts and Graphs." *Applied Cognitive Psychology* 3 (1989): 185–226.

Landels, J. G. *Engineering in the Ancient World*. Berkeley: U of California P, 1978.

Lécuyer, Bernard, and Anthony R. Oberschall. "The Early History of Social Research." *International Encyclopedia of the Social Sciences*. New York: Free, 1968.

Lippmann, Walter. *Public Opinion*. New York: Macmillan, 1927.

Littleton, A. C. *Accounting Evolution to 1900*. 1933. University: U of Alabama P, 1981.

Macdonald-Ross, M. "How Numbers Are Shown: A Review of Research on the Presentation of Quantitative Data in Texts." *Audio-Visual Communication Review* 25 (1977): 359–407.

Monmonier, Mark. *How to Lie with Maps*. Chicago: U of Chicago P, 1991.

———. *Maps with the News*. Chicago: U of Chicago P, 1989.

Mukerji, Chandra. *From Graven Images: Patterns of Modern Materialism*. New York: Columbia UP, 1983.

National Assessment of Educational Progress. *Reading: Graphic Materials (Theme 2)*. Washington: GPO, 1973.

Nodley, Rudolf, and Dyno Lowenstein. *Pictographs and Graphs: How to Make and Use Them*. New York: Harper, 1952.

Pasternack, Steve, and Sandra H. Utt. "Reader Use and Understanding of Newspaper Informational Graphics." *Newspaper Research Journal* 12.3 (1990): 28–41.

Peel, E. A. "Generalizing Through the Verbal Medium." *British Journal of Educational Psychology* 48 (1978): 36–46.

Porter, Theodore M. *The Rise of Statistical Thinking, 1820–1900*. Princeton: Princeton UP, 1986.

Radicati, Carlos de Primeglio. *El Sistema Contable de los Incas*. Lima: Studium, n.d.

Rising, James S., Maurice W. Almfeldt, and Paul S. DeJong. *Engineering Graphics*. 5th ed. Dubuque: Kendall, 1977.

Robinson, Arthur H. *Early Thematic Mapping in the History of Cartography*. Chicago: U of Chicago P, 1982.

Rogers, Anna C. *Graphic Charts Handbook*. Washington: Public Affairs P, 1961.

Roller, Beverly V. "Graph Reading Abilities of Thirteen-Year-Olds." *Processing of Visible Language*. Ed. P. A. Kolers, M. E. Wrolstad, and H. Bouma. Vol. 1. New York: Plenum, 1980. 305–14.

Schmid, C. F. *Statistical Graphics*. New York: Wiley, 1983.

Snell, Daniel C. *Ledgers and Prices: Early Mesopotamian Merchant Accounts*. New Haven: Yale UP, 1982.

Steidel, Robert F., Jr., and Jerald M. Henderson. *The Graphic*

Languages of Engineering. New York: Wiley, 1983.

Stigler, Stephen M. *The History of Statistics.* Cambridge: Harvard UP, 1986.

Sullivan, Peter. *Newspaper Graphics.* Darmstadt: IFRA, 1987.

Susman, Warren I. *Culture as History: The Transformation of American Society in the Twentieth Century.* New York: Pantheon, 1984.

Taylor, Shelley E., and Suzanne C. Thompson. "Stalking the Elusive 'Vividness' Effect." *Psychological Review* 89 (1982): 155–81.

Terrell, Pamela M. "Newspaper Art Enters a New Era." *Presstime* Feb. 1989: 20–27.

Tooley, R. V. *Maps and Map-Makers.* 7th ed. London: Batsford, 1987.

Tufte, Edward R. *Envisioning Information.* Cheshire: Privately printed, 1990.

————. *The Visual Display of Quantitative Information.* Cheshire: Privately printed, 1983.

White, Jan V. *Using Charts and Graphs: One-Thousand Ways to Visual Persuasion.* New York: Bowker, 1984.

————. "Visual Persuasion." *Folio* Oct. 1984: 97–104.

Wildbur, Peter. *Information Graphics.* New York: Van Nostrand, 1989.

Wilford, John Noble. *The Mapmakers.* New York: Knopf, 1981.

Wood, Denis. "Pleasure in the Idea: The Atlas as Narrative Form." *Cartographica* 24.1 (1987): 24–45.

Wood, Denis, with John Fels. *The Power of Maps.* New York: Guilford, 1992.

Wood, Denis, and John Fels. "Designs on Signs: Myth and Meaning in Maps." *Cartographica* 23.3 (1986): 54–103.

◈

CHAPTER 4
INTERPRETING TYPOGRAPHY

Amert, Kay. "Origins of the French Old-Style: The Roman and Italic Types of Simon de Colines." *Printing History* 26/27 13.1/14.2 (1991–92): 17–40.

Anderson, Donald. *The Art of Written Forms: The Theory and Practice of Calligraphy.* New York: Holt, 1969.

Barnhurst, Kevin G. "The Great American Newspaper." *American Scholar* 60 (Winter 1991): 106–12.

Barnhurst , Kevin G., and John C. Nerone. "Design Trends in U.S. Front Pages, 1885–1985." *Journalism Quarterly* 68 (1992): 796–804.

Barnhurst, Kevin G., and Ellen Wartella. "Newspapers and Citizenship:

Young Adults' Subjective Experience of Newspapers." *Critical Studies in Mass Communication* 8 (1991): 195–209.

Brinton, James E. "The 'Feeling' of Type Faces." *Journal of Commercial Art and Design* 3.10 (1961): 43–45.

Carter, Harry. *A View of Early Typography*. Oxford: Clarendon, 1969.

Carter, Sebastian. *Twentieth Century Type Designers*. New York: Taplinger, 1987.

Catich, Edward M. *The Origin of the Serif: Brush Writing and Roman Letters*. Davenport: Catfish, 1968.

Chappell, Warren. *A Short History of the Printed Word*. 1970. New York: Dorset, 1989.

Chartier, Roger, ed. *The Culture of Print: Power and the Uses of Print in Early Modern Europe*. Trans. Lydia G. Cochrane. Cambridge: Polity, 1989.

Craig, Robert L. "On the Aesthetics of Typographic Style." Unpublished essay, 1992.

———. "Designing Ethnicity: The Ideology of Images." *Design Issues* 7.2 (1991): 34–42.

Deuchler, Florens. *Gothic*. Trans. Vivienne Menkes. The Universe History of Art and Architecture. New York: Universe, 1989.

Diringer, David. *The Alphabet: A Key to the History of Mankind*. 3rd ed. New York: Funk, 1968.

Eisenstein, Elizabeth L. *The Printing Press as an Agent of Change: Communications and Cultural Transformations in Early Modern Europe*. 2 vols. Cambridge: Cambridge UP, 1979.

———. *The Printing Revolution in Early Modern Europe*. New York: Cambridge UP, 1983.

Elam, Kimberly. *Expressive Typography: The Word as Image*. New York: Van Nostrand, 1990.

Goldberg, Jonathan. *Writing Matter: From the Hands of the English Renaissance*. Stanford: Stanford UP, 1990.

Goudy, Frederick W. *The Alphabet and Elements of Lettering*. 1942. Berkeley: U of California P, 1952.

———. *Typologia: Studies in Type Design and Type Making*. Berkeley: U of California P, 1940.

Harum, Albert E. *Typography and Newspaper Makeup*. Dubuque: Brown, 1951.

Humez, Alexander, and Nicholas Humez. *Alpha to Omega: The Life and Times of the Greek Alphabet*. Boston: Godine, 1981.

Hutt, Allen. *The Changing Newspaper: Typographic Trends in Britain and America, 1622–1972*. London: Fraser, 1973.

Innis, Harold A. *Empire and Communications*. 1950. Toronto: U of Toronto P, 1972.

Jackson, Donald. *The Story of Writing*. New York: Taplinger, 1981.

Johnson, A. F. *Type Designs: Their History and Development.* 3rd ed. London: Deutsch, 1967.

Kastl, Albert J., and Irvin L. Child. "Emotional Meaning of Four Typographical Variables." *Journal of Applied Psychology* 52 (1968): 440–46.

Lawson, Alexander S. *Anatomy of a Typeface.* Boston: Godine, 1990.

———. *Printing Types: An Introduction.* Boston: Beacon, 1971.

Luckiesh, Matthew. *Light, Vision and Seeing.* New York: Van Nostrand, 1944.

McLuhan, Marshall. *The Gutenberg Galaxy: The Making of Typographic Man.* Toronto: U of Toronto P, 1962.

Meggs, Philip B. *A History of Graphic Design.* New York: Van Nostrand, 1983.

Moran, James. *Stanley Morison: His Typographic Achievement.* London: Lund Humphries, 1971.

Morison, Stanley. *The English Newspaper.* Cambridge, Eng.: Cambridge UP, 1932.

———. *First Principles of Typography.* New York: Macmillan, 1936.

———. *Politics and Script: Aspects of Authority and Freedom in the Development of Graeco-Latin Script from the Sixth Century B.C. to the Twentieth Century A.D.* Ed. Nicolas Barker. Oxford: Clarendon, 1972.

———. *Printing the* Times *since 1785.* London: Times, 1953.

Morison, Stanley, and Holbrook Jackson. *A Brief Survey of Printing: History and Practice.* London: Fleuron, 1923.

Nolan, Barbara. *The Gothic Visionary Perspective.* Princeton: Princeton UP, 1977.

Ovink, G. *Legibility, Atmosphere-Value and Forms of Printing Types.* Leiden: Sijthoff, 1938.

Patterson, Donald G., and Miles A. Tinker. *How to Make Type Readable: A Manual for Typographers, Printers and Advertisers.* New York: Harper, 1940.

Perfect, Christopher, and Gordon Rookledge. *Rookledge's International Type-Finder.* London: Sarema, 1983.

Pyke, R. L. *Report on the Legibility of Print.* London: HMSO, 1926.

Rehe, Rolf F. *Typography: How to Make It Most Legible.* Carmel: Design Research International, 1984.

Ruder, Emil. *Typography: A Manual of Design.* New York: Hastings, 1967.

Ruegg, Ruedi, and Godi Frohlich. *Basic Typography.* Zurich: ABC, 1972.

Spencer, Herbert. *Pioneers of Modern Typography.* 2nd ed. London: Lund, 1982.

————. *The Visible Word*. New York: Hastings, 1969.

Swann, Cal. *Language and Typography*. New York: Van Nostrand, 1991.

Tinker, M. A. *Legibility of Print*. Ames: Iowa State UP, 1963.

Tschichold, Jan. *Asymmetric Typography*. Trans. Ruari McLean. New York: Reinhold, 1967.

Updike, Daniel Berkeley. *Printing Types, Their History, Forms, and Use: A Study in Survivals*. Cambridge: Belknap-Harvard UP, 1962.

Warde, Beatrice. *The Crystal Goblet: Sixteen Essays on Typography*. Ed. Henry Jacob. Cleveland: World, 1956.

Warner, Michael. "The Public Sphere and the Cultural Mediation of Print." *Ruthless Criticism: New Perspectives in U.S. Communication History*. Ed. William S. Solomon and Robert W. McChesney. Minneapolis: U of Minnesota P, 1993.

White, Hayden. *Metahistory: The Historical Imagination in Nineteenth-Century Europe*. Baltimore: Johns Hopkins UP, 1973.

Whitehill, Clayton. *The Moods of Type*. New York: Barnes, 1947.

Wolfflin, Heinrich. *Principles of Art History: The Problem of the Development of Style in Later Art*. 1932. New York: Dover, 1950.

Zachrisson, Bror. *Studies in Legibility*. Stockholm: Almqvist, 1965.

CHAPTER 5
EVALUATING LAYOUT

Allen, John E. *Newspaper Designing*. New York: Harper, 1947.

American Press Institute. *Newspaper Design 2000 and Beyond*. Reston: API, 1988.

Arnold, Edmund C. *Functional Newspaper Design*. New York: Harper, 1956.

Baird, Russell N., Duncan McDonald, Ronald H. Pittman, and Arthur Turnbull. *The Graphics of Communication*. 6th ed. New York: Harcourt, 1993.

Barnhurst, Kevin G. "Contemporary Terrorism in Peru: Sendero Luminoso and the Media." *Journal of Communication* 41 (1991): 75–89.

————. "Layout as Political Expression: The Press and Sendero Luminoso." Unpublished manuscript, 1990.

————. "News as Art." *Journalism Monographs* 130 (1991).

Barnhurst, Kevin G., and Alan L. Ellis. "Effects of Modern and Postmodern Design Styles on Reader Perceptions of News." *Visual Communication: Bridging across Cultures*. Ed. J. Clark-Baca,

D. G. Beauchamp, and R. A. Braden. Blacksburg: IVLA, 1992. 15–24.

Barnhurst, Kevin G., and John C. Nerone. "Design Trends in U.S. Front Pages, 1885–1985." *Journalism Quarterly* 68 (1992): 796–804.

Berger, John. *Ways of Seeing.* London: BBC and Penguin, 1972.

Bragdon, Claude. "The Arithmetic of Beauty." *The Beautiful Necessity.* Rochester: Manus, 1910. 91–100.

Brucker, Herbert. *The Changing American Newspaper.* New York: Columbia UP, 1937.

Caputi, Jane. "Charting the Flow: The Construction of Meaning through Juxtaposition in Media Texts." *Journal of Communication Inquiry* 15 (1991): 32–47.

Chappell, Warren. *A Short History of the Printed Word.* 1970. New York: Dorset, 1989.

Chartier, Roger, ed. *The Culture of Print: Power and the Uses of Print in Early Modern Europe.* Trans. Lydia G. Cochrane. Cambridge: Polity, 1989.

Click, J. W., and Guido H. Stempel III. "Reader Response to Modern and Traditional Front Page Make-Up." *ANPA News Research Bulletin* no. 4 (June 1974).

Craig, Robert. "Ideological Aspects of Publication Design." *Design Issues* 6.2 (1990): 18–27.

De Lopatecki, Eugene. *Advertising Layout and Typography.* New York: Ronald, 1935.

Dondis, Donis A. *A Primer of Visual Literacy.* Cambridge: MIT P, 1973.

Emery, Edwin. *The Press and America.* Englewood Cliffs: Prentice, 1954.

Evans, Harold. *Newspaper Design.* Editing and Design 5. New York: Holt, 1973.

Feinberg, Howard L., and Bruce D. Itule. *Visual Editing: A Graphic Guide for Journalists.* Belmont: Wadsworth, 1990.

Fisher, J. L. "Art Styles as Cultural Cognitive Maps." *American Anthropologist* 63 (1961): 79–93.

Ganje, Lucy A. "Design of the Native Press: A Cultural Perspective." Unpublished paper, 1992.

García, Mario R. *Contemporary Newspaper Design: A Structural Approach.* 2nd ed. Englewood Cliffs: Prentice, 1987.

Gentry, James K., and Barbara Zang. "Newspapers' New Face: The Graphics Editor Takes Charge." *Washington Journalism Review* Jan./Feb. 1989: 24–28.

Hall, Edward T. *The Hidden Dimension.* New York: Anchor, 1966.

———. *The Silent Language.* New York: Anchor, 1959.

Hurlburt, Allen. *The Grid: A Modular System for the Design and*

Production of Newspapers, Magazines, and Books. New York: Van Nostrand, 1978.

Hutt, Allen. *The Changing Newspaper: Typographic Trends in Britain and America, 1622–1972*. London: Fraser, 1973.

Jones, Michael Wynn. *Deadline Disaster: A Newspaper History*. Chicago: Regnery, 1976.

Lauer, David A. *Design Basics*. New York: Holt, 1979.

Le Corbusier. *The Modulor*. Cambridge: Harvard UP, 1954.

Lockwood, Robert. *News by Design*. Denver: Quark, 1992.

Manevy, Raymond. *L'Evolution des formules de présentation de la presse quotidienne*. Paris: Córrea, 1956.

Martin, Richard O. "The Nonverbal 'Language' of Typographic Layout." *Journalism Abstracts* 2 (1964): 18–20.

Meggs, Philip B. *A History of Graphic Design*. New York: Van Nostrand, 1983.

Moen, Daryl R. *Newspaper Layout and Design*. Ames: Iowa State UP, 1984.

Moriarty, Sandra E., and Lisa Rohe. "Cultural Palettes: An Exercise in Sensitivity for Designers." *Journalism Educator* 46.4 (1992): 32–37.

Morison, Stanley. *The English Newspaper*. Cambridge, Eng.: Cambridge UP, 1932.

———. *The Origins of the Newspaper*. London: Times, 1954.

Mott, Frank Luther. *American Journalism*. New York: Macmillan, 1941.

Nelson, Roy Paul. *Publication Design*. Dubuque: Brown, 1983.

Nerone, John C. "The Problem of Teaching Journalism History." *Journalism Educator* 45.3 (1990): 16–24.

Ong, Walter J. *Orality and Literacy*. London: New Accents, 1982.

Osborn, Alex F. *A Short Course in Advertising*. New York: Scribner's, 1921.

O'Shaughnessy, James. *Easy to Read: Philosophy of Typography*. New York: Brevier, 1928.

Rand, Paul. *Thoughts on Design*. New York: Wittenborn, Schultz, 1947.

Roshan, Maer. "Guilt by Life Style." *New York Times* 19 Jan. 1992, nat. ed.: A25.

Sandage, Charles H. *Advertising Theory and Practice*. 1936. Chicago: Business, 1939.

Schudson, Michael. *Discovering the News: A Social History of American Newspapers*. New York: Harper, 1978.

Scott, Robert G. *Design Fundamentals*. New York: McGraw, 1951.

Society of Newspaper Design. *First Edition: The Best of Newspaper Design* (annual). New York: Newsweek, 1981.

Starch, Daniel. *Principles of Advertising*. New York: McGraw, 1923.

Steinberg, S. H. *Five Hundred Years of Printing*. Middlesex:

Penguin, 1955.

Wallace, Allen. *A Design for News*. Minneapolis: Star, 1981.

Wilkerson, Isabel. "One City's 30-Year Crusade for Integration." *New York Times* 30 Dec. 1991, nat. ed.: A1, 11.

Williams, Keith. *The English Newspaper: An Illustrated History to 1900*. London: Springwood, 1977.

Young, Frank H. *Technique of Advertising Layout*. New York: Covici Friede, 1935.

Acknowledgments (continued from copyright page)

Figure 2.9, courtesy of *The Virginian-Pilot* and *Ledger-Star*.

Figure 2.10, courtesy of Hal Fischer.

Figure 3.1, reprinted with permission of *The Detroit News*, a Gannett newspaper, copyright © 1991.

Figure 3.2, After Burner is a trademark of SEGA. Copyright © 1993 SEGA. All rights reserved.

Figure 3.3, courtesy of Biblioteca Nazionale Marciana.

Figure 3.4, from Daniel C. Snell, *Ledgers and Prices: Early Mesopotamian Merchant Accounts* (New Haven: Yale University Press, 1982), pl. xv. Copyright Yale University Press.

Figure 3.7, courtesy of Service Photographique de la Bibliothèque Nationale.

Figure 3.12, from the U.S. Department of Agriculture/Department of Health and Human Services.

Figure 3.13, copyrighted 1993, Chicago Tribune Company, all rights reserved, used with permission.

Figure 4.3, courtesy of Father Edward M. Catich, St. Ambrose University.

Figure 4.14, all rights reserved, The Metropolitan Museum of Art.

Figure 4.15, reprinted with permission of Linotype-Hell Company.

Figure 4.17, © Times Newspapers Ltd. 1993.

Figure 4.18, from Morison, *The English Newspaper* (New York: Cambridge University Press, 1932), p. 7. Copyright 1932 by Cambridge University Press and used with permission.

Figure 4.21, courtesy of *The Virginian-Pilot* and *Ledger-Star*.

Figure 4.22, reprinted with the permission of the *Chicago Sun-Times*, © 1993.

Figure 4.23, used with permission from the *New York Post*, August 5, 1938, and with permission of Vis-Com Inc.

Figure 4.24, reprinted with permission of the *Boston Herald*.

Figure 5.1, courtesy of *The Times* of London. © Times Newspapers Ltd. 1993.

Figure 5.5, reprinted with permission of Linotype-Hell Company.

Figure 5.6, from De Lopatecki, Eugene, *Advertising Layout and Typography* (New York: Ronald, 1935), pp. 16, 28, 37, 45, 53.

Figure 5.7, reprinted with permission of the Los Angeles Times Syndicate.

Figure 5.8, reprinted with permission of Vis-Com Inc.

Figure 5.9, reprinted with permission of Vignelli Associates.

Figure 5.10, reprinted with permission of the *Star Tribune*, Minneapolis–St. Paul.

Figure 5.13, reprinted with permission of *El Comercio*.

Figure 5.14, reprinted with permission of *Exponent II*.

Figure 5.15, reprinted with permission of *Emigre Magazine*.

INDEX

Italicized page numbers refer to figures.